"In his straight-forward, tell-it-like-it-is style, author and Ohio native David Murray offers his personal and professional insight into how communication is a tool for all of us—not so much as politicians, business leaders, parents, or friends, but just as humans to better understand each other and ourselves. Through anecdotes, stories, and personal experience, Murray teaches us that *how* we talk is as important as *what* we say. Sharp, witty, and entertaining, *Effort to Understand* is a fun—but equally instructive—read!"

—**MIKE DEWINE**, **Governor of Ohio**

"In an America divided by race and religion, class and culture, identity and ideology, David Murray urges us all to make 'an effort to understand' each other. With decades of experience in organizational communications, Murray examines public speeches, from political candidates to corporate CEOs, for clues to how we all can better express ourselves and empathize with friends, family members, coworkers, and fellow citizens. And he enriches his analysis with engaging stories from work-life, parenthood, and Chicago life."

—**DAVID KUSNET**, **chief speechwriter for President Bill Clinton and author of *Speaking American***

"In these hyperpartisan and polarized times, Americans interested in building bridges to each other rather than forever manning the ramparts can find no better instruction than the intelligent, absorbing new book by veteran communications expert David Murray. A smart and persuasive guide for how to communicate effectively to political opposites."

—**MARK SALTER**, **author of *The Luckiest Man: Life with John McCain***

"The ultimate communicator's analysis of how to bridge the gaps in our understanding of each other, no matter how great the divide. We just need the right phrases at the right moment. And the ability to listen—really listen. Reassuring, insightful, practical, and wise, David Murray serves up an insider's guide to our better selves and the words that can lead the way there."

—**VIV GROSKOP**, **author of *How to Own the Room: Women and the Art of Brilliant Speaking***

"Whenever David published one of my speeches in *Vital Speeches of the Day*, it always felt like validation that I had gotten it right. In this collection of his own writing, David gets it exactly right—if we as a nation are to heal, we need to make an effort to understand all the things we have in common, and relate to how and why we differ. This collection of essays is for the people who won't give up the hope that we can."

—**JAMES R. CLAPPER**, **former director of National Intelligence**

"*An Effort to Understand* is compelling, instructive, inspirational, and timely. David Murray's reflections on communication—by leaders, among citizens, and between friends and family members—come at a time when it is clear that forthright, civil, and thoughtful communication is desperately needed. David helped a gifted, talented battlefield colleague of mine, who received a fatal medical diagnosis, write the *New York Times* best seller *Tell My Sons* before my comrade died, and he has helped countless others over the years, as well. Now David writes over his name on one of the most pressing issues of the day—the need for all of us to engage each other respectfully, thoughtfully, and openly. His words could not be more important."

—**GENERAL DAVID PETRAEUS, former commander of the surge in Iraq, US Central Command, and Coalition Forces in Afghanistan, and former director of the CIA**

"Whether you are a staunch Democrat who starts the day with *Morning Joe* or a firm Republican who begins the morning with the folks on the white couch on *Fox & Friends*, you know that part of being a patriot is listening to the differing views of fellow citizens. In this most American book, writer David Murray teaches you how to make your own truly honest *Effort to Understand.*"

—**ADMIRAL JAMES G. STAVRIDIS (Ret.), former European Supreme Allied Commander, NATO**

"David Murray says great communication requires great listening. He may not be the first to make this observation, but he may be the only one to explain how to do it: with focus, intent and goodwill. Sounds straightforward, but few explain it so clearly. And fewer of us actually do it. We live in a time of polarization. Research makes clear we don't even talk to people with differing political views. That's a problem for each of us and for our country. I hope everyone reads David's compelling book and applies the lessons in real life. We'll be better off for it."

—**BOB FELDMAN, founder, The Dialogue Project**

"This is high-level entertainment that will improve your moral character. It is a wonderful defense of truth telling in our sordid post-truth time."

—**TOM GEOGHEGAN, labor lawyer and author of *Which Side Are You On: Trying to Be for Labor When It's Flat on Its Back***

AN
EFFORT TO
UNDERSTAND

AN
EFFORT TO
UNDERSTAND

Hearing One Another (and Ourselves)
in a Nation Cracked in Half

———

Essays from a Life in American Communication

DAVID
MURRAY

DISRUPTION
BOOKS

AUSTIN   NEW YORK

Published by Disruption Books
New York, NY
www.disruptionbooks.com

Distributed by Disruption Books

For ordering information or special discounts for bulk purchases, please contact Disruption Books at info@disruptionbooks.com.

Library of Congress Cataloging-in-Publication Data
Names: Murray, David, (speechwriter) author.
Title: An effort to understand : hearing one another (and ourselves) in a nation cracked in half / David Murray.
Description: First edition. | New York : Disruption Books, 2021. | Summary: "What we say, what we don't, and why it matters. This new collection of essays from rhetoric authority and celebrated writing blogger David Murray applies his signature blend of humor and heart to a free-wheeling conversation about how we communicate in America. With essays like 'We Deserve Leaders Who Act Like They Like Us,' and 'Speaking Truth to Power: Talking to Myself,' Murray's words give readers a window into everyday American discourse—from the backroads of rural Illinois to the carpeted halls of the C-suite. Guided by an ear for the lessons of history, *An Effort to Understand* shows that the personal and political gulfs between us are small compared to our common desire to connect. American discord is nothing new, but we have a chance at trust, peace, and solidarity if we make an effort to speak more honestly and listen to understand."—Provided by publisher.
Identifiers: LCCN 2020032602 | ISBN 9781633310483 (trade paperback) | ISBN 9781633310490 (epub)
Subjects: LCSH: Communication—Social aspects—United States. | Communication—Political aspects —United States. | Communication and culture—United States. | Interpersonal communication—United States.
Classification: LCC HM1206 .M88 2021 | DDC 302.2—dc23
LC record available at https://lccn.loc.gov/2020032602

Print ISBN: 978-1-63331-048-3
eBook ISBN: 978-1-63331-049-0

Cover and text design by Kimberly Lance

First Edition

To the communicators.

Contents

What Is "An Effort to Understand"?

"Do they know about Martin Luther King?"

You can hear Senator Robert F. Kennedy ask someone this as he stands on the back of a flatbed truck in the early-spring dark, on a street corner in a park in an all-Black neighborhood in North Indianapolis.

You can just make out the answer of a white official: "We have left it up to you."

Kennedy hesitates for exactly two seconds, and then makes a request that must have come to members of the ebullient crowd as the first signal that this was not going to be a typical campaign rally.

"Could you lower those signs, please?"

Another two seconds.

"I have some very sad news for all of you . . . and that is that Martin Luther King was shot and was killed tonight in Memphis, Tennessee."

The whole crowd screams at once, then grows quiet just as quickly, which might have surprised Kennedy. He waits nine seconds before beginning again.

> Martin Luther King dedicated his life to love and to justice between fellow human beings. He died in the cause of that effort. In this difficult day, in this difficult time for the United States, it's perhaps well to ask what kind of a nation we are, and what direction we want to move in.

That was April 4, 1968, about a year before I was born.

Hundreds of times, I've listened to the speech that Kennedy went on to deliver that night. I've shown it to audiences of writers all over the United States and all over the world. Every time I've shown it, it has meant something more to me. And every year, it seems to me less a relic of America's past and more a haunting prediction of America's future.

The speech is only five minutes long, and 543 words. When you hear a speech that short that many times over a period of time, different words begin to get under your skin and start to itch:

> We can move in that direction as a country, in greater polarization—Black people amongst Blacks, white amongst whites, filled with hatred toward one another. Or we can make an effort, as Martin Luther King did, to understand and to comprehend, and replace that violence, that stain of bloodshed that has spread across our land, with an effort to understand, compassion and love.

That phrase: *an effort to understand.* A little later he repeats it again: "But we have to make an effort in the United States. We have to make an effort to understand." It sounds so bland. So obvious. So preachy. So white.

So why did he say it three times to an all-Black crowd reeling in shock and despair?

And why did they listen?

————

My fascination with Robert Kennedy began with a story about his own assassination, only two months later—told to me by my mother when I was very young. Kennedy was shot after a midnight celebration of his victory in the California primary. My mother learned the news in the morning through her clock radio. In the 1960s, clock radios were a big thing.

Instead of a harsh ring or tone for your alarm, the radio would come on. The news must've crept in through her sleep that night, because she remembered waking up already crying. "For Bobby," she explained to me.

What kind of politician could make my intellectual, often sardonic mother cry like that? Who could make her call him Bobby?

My interest in Kennedy's Indianapolis speech, on the other hand, was professional at first. As the editor of a magazine called *Vital Speeches of the Day*, I was getting invited by groups of professional speechwriters and other communicators to give speeches about what makes speeches great. I soon figured out it was good to show clips from speeches, so audiences could see and hear and feel what I was talking about. Kennedy's speech had a few advantages: It was short, and I could show the whole thing. It also had a subtly sophisticated structure, and it achieved a lot, rhetorically speaking, in just a few minutes' time. And it was old enough that it didn't divide my audience along political lines.

And Kennedy's Indianapolis speech added one more benefit to my lectures, in the heroic stories that bookended it: Beforehand, Kennedy had insisted on showing up to deliver the speech even though all his advisors had cautioned against it and the local police had refused to give him an escort. And afterward? That night every major city in America burned with riots—except Indianapolis, where Bobby Kennedy had called for peace.

Speechwriters appreciate that tidy grace note. If you write speeches for a living, you like to think that a speech has the power to make good things happen, all by itself. But that story seemed a little too immaculate to me, even just in terms of logistics: a five-minute speech in a little park on the north side of Indianapolis prevented a whole city from rioting?

Eventually, that became another itch I wanted to scratch.

For an article I was writing to mark the fiftieth anniversary of MLK's death and Kennedy's speech, in 2018, a friend and I drove from Chicago to

Indianapolis, to see the spot where that flatbed truck had been parked—
and to try to find someone who had been there that night. There's a really
wonderful sculpture at the corner, showing Kennedy and King reaching
toward one another across a sidewalk. The neighborhood is still mostly
Black, still pretty poor. Kountry Kitchen Soul Food Place is within walking distance, and we ate lunch there and asked a few old-timers about
April 4, 1968. One said he knew a guy who had been there that night, and
who was now in city politics. I got the guy's number, and when I returned
home to Chicago, I called him up.

Indianapolis City Councilman William Oliver was willing to talk
about that night, but like the overwhelming majority of Black residents of
Indianapolis, he hadn't been at Kennedy's rally. Still, he gave me exactly
what I needed.

A twenty-eight-year-old screw machine operator at the local Chrysler
plant in 1968, Oliver was actually at another political rally three miles
across town, this one for Congressman Andrew Jacobs, who was running
for reelection, backed by the United Auto Workers union. Oliver was
aware that Kennedy was in town, but he wouldn't have attended the Kennedy rally anyhow, because it was located in a neighborhood unfriendly
to the neighborhood he grew up in: "I had no business going there, and
they had no business going where I was."

And anyway, Oliver said to me, "Who was Bobby Kennedy?" All he
knew about the Kennedys as a kid was that it seemed as though they were
"kind of procrastinating about civil rights in the South."

As a matter of fact, Martin Luther King hadn't exactly mesmerized
young Oliver either. King was maligned in the local Indianapolis papers
for being disruptive on one hand and ineffective on the other, and Oliver was influenced by those views. He thinks a lot more people—even
Black people—claim to have marched with King, whether literally or fig-
uratively, than actually did. But as Oliver describes the night he learned
King was killed—when word spread through the crowd at the Jacobs
rally "and the women started wailing"—he recalls a feeling of "emptiness,

like, 'They . . . they . . . have taken something away from us. One of the few good things about the whole world was this Martin King. Is he really gone?' It took our hope away."

As Oliver said to me, "I didn't know he was here—until he was gone."

In any case, Oliver is annoyed that Robert Kennedy gets credit for calming down Indianapolis that night. He remembers many times since then in his life when racial unrest begat violence in various American cities. For local cultural reasons that Oliver doesn't understand, Indianapolis's Black community never resorted, he said, to "burnin' down the town."

Kennedy?

No, said Oliver. "He didn't do this."

Every April 4, Oliver attends a remembrance at the site of the speech, along with a few hundred other Indianapolis residents. It seems to him that each year, Kennedy's speech gets more emphasis and Martin Luther King's life gets less. And Oliver thinks to himself, *Wait a minute. We're making a monument out of someone who just passed on the information.*

Of course, Kennedy did much more with that speech than pass on the news of King's death. Oliver confessed to me he'd never actually seen the whole speech before. I sent him a YouTube link and asked him to watch it. He watched it twice. "I would appreciate it today," he told me afterward. "I can feel every word of that now, and it almost makes me want to tear up."

The day after his speech in Indianapolis, with the help of his speech-writers, Kennedy gave a more formal, more philosophical version at the City Club of Cleveland. "We must admit the vanity of our false distinctions among men and learn to find our own advancement in the search for the advancement of all," he said.

> We must recognize that this short life can neither be ennobled or enriched by hatred or revenge . . . that those who live with us are our brothers, that they share with us the same short movement of life, that they seek—as we do—nothing

but the chance to live out their lives in purpose and happiness, winning what satisfaction and fulfillment they can.

What was Oliver doing on April 5, while Kennedy was addressing white men in suits over dessert at the City Club luncheon? "What day of the week was it?" he asked me. It was a Friday. He probably went to work at the Chrysler plant.

———

Tonight in the park where Robert F. Kennedy called for understanding a half century ago, Kennedy and Martin Luther King, their words still ringing out on YouTube, reach out to each other in perpetuity. As I reached out to William Oliver, and as the city councilman reached back out to me. As we must all reach out to one another and make an effort to understand, in our own difficult time now in the United States.

But of course my phone conversation with Oliver was too little, and fifty years too late. Am I able to travel back in time and tell a young Black screw machine operator that he should be more attuned, over the din of the late 1960s, to this particular Kennedy's gentle words, sincerely offered and courageously delivered? No more than I can go back and hasten a young Bobby Kennedy's plodding spiritual journey to social enlightenment—which also came too late, both for him and for the rest of the nation.

Surely our own effort to understand one another is just as urgent. Will it, also, be too little and too late? That's up to us: me and you.

Communication requires listening as much as speaking. It requires deep listening and constant listening. It requires careful listening, imaginative listening, and repeated listening. And in our own time, if we are going to have a society that is worth living in, we must learn to truly listen, to hear. We must sense—with the tiniest cilia of our ears and the tenderest membranes of our hearts—not just the words of our friends and family, our coworkers and leaders, but the deepest intent of those words and their emotional source. We must listen with the assumption, so hard to sustain in the daily madness of American life, that the other person came by his or her views as honestly (or maybe as dishonestly) as we came to ours. And we must listen with the belief that with an effort, we can understand.

That's communication, and that's what this book is about. In these pages, I talk about my own evolution—from a writer who tried to draw crowds around my work by using words to start fights, to a communicator who gives most of my energy and talents to cultivating lots of rich, common soil where people can gather in peaceful productivity.

In these pages, I urge readers to join me in a near-spiritual movement toward thinking of communication as more than a means of persuading others to our way of thinking, but as a way of thinking all its own—and indeed a way of life. I describe how the leaders in our lives ought to communicate, and I suggest what those leaders need from us. I talk politics: how we can all engage with one another more honestly on fraught subjects, and why we must do so. And I talk about how we can communicate more productively with our colleagues, more lovingly with our friends and family, and more thoughtfully with acquaintances and strangers.

This is not a call for "civility"; in fact, that concept gets a spanking in here. We will always have trouble in America, and we will always have discord. But I believe that Americans can have more peace when we crave it, more solidarity when we require it, and more trust when it comes right down to it—in every aspect of our American lives.

I believe that even the most politically opposed or culturally estranged or emotionally isolated Americans share vastly more common experience and values than we know—a reality we would become more consciously aware of if we redirected some of the intellectual energy we use to draw distinctions and describe our differences, and instead we applied that energy to see one another more clearly. And we would see ourselves more clearly as a result. As another Kennedy said—and as we were so brutally reminded in the coronavirus spring of 2020—"in the final analysis, our most basic common link is that we all inhabit this small planet. We all breathe the same air. We all cherish our children's future. And we are all mortal."

Can we always understand? Maybe not.

But we can always make an effort to understand.

I've been writing these essays not just since President Trump was elected, but since President Obama was elected. We think of this as a uniquely divided moment, but do you remember the 2008 election, won by a man who—according to a large chunk of the country—was some combination of communist, terrorist, and malevolent foreign national?

I was live-blogging on Election Night 2008 from my condo in Chicago, in happy anticipation: "It's 6:00 p.m. Central time. I'm on the couch next to my wife, in my pajamas, with a load of pad Thai on the way, a bottle of red wine on the coffee table, and in case of a nasty surprise, a thirty-pack of Pabst in the refrigerator."

One of my very best friends, who hated Obama for reasons of his own, emailed to say that I was "tiresome and gross," and that he hoped I'd choke on the pad Thai. I published his email on the blog, with his name on it. Things were never the same between us after that, and I haven't seen him in many years. (I did text him on the eve of Chicago's official order to shelter in place to tell him I love him. He returned the sentiment, and we promised to get together as soon as we can. We've made this vow before. Perhaps this time it will stick.)

So it's been a long twelve years in America. It's been a long fifty years in America. Indeed, it's been a long 244 years in America. The question is, will it be a long future for a nation that's worthy of the pride that all of us— even the most discouraged—feel at the very sound of the word *America*?

To answer that question, you have to take the long view. I've developed these ideas over three decades in and around journalism, oral history, public relations, leadership, and psychology. And as you're about to learn, my soapbox is the shoulders of the wise writers who raised me, the giant humanists whom I've been lucky enough to count as mentors, and the hundreds of professional communicators I have called my colleagues. All these people have given their whole lives to communication—to the essential idea that with sincere intent and real imagination, all human beings can understand one another. As Harold said to Maude in the classic film *Harold and Maude*, "You sure have a way with people." And as Maude replied, "Well, they're my species!"

I have taken every bit of wisdom I can from all these people. And this is the sum total, so far, of one man's life in communication, in today's America.

I hope you are able to put some of it to use in your life—for the good of our species and our life together.

I.

LIFE,
COMMUNICATED

I was raised to be a communicator. My parents were both writers by trade—my mother an advertising copywriter and literary novelist, my father an advertising creative director and an essayist. Even with the commercials they made, they wanted to reach across the divides, racial and generational, of their time.

My mother wrote a newspaper ad in 1964. "If you feel sure civil rights is moving fast enough," began the headline over a grainy black-and-white photograph of a racially ambiguous child in a crib, "try to imagine your children waking up Negro tomorrow morning."

A few years later, my father articulated his communication philosophy in a memo whose terms are as dated as its title—"The Man Inside the Man"—but whose message holds:

> All of us, as human beings, wear a protective cover or a kind of year-round Halloween mask to keep our nerve endings hidden, to keep our soft underside of hopes and needs and hang-ups, our fears, our pride and prejudices, our irrationalities and our cry buttons from hanging right out there in the sunlight for someone to push in or puncture. And it's this paper-thin shell that confuses a lot of people in advertising. It's this shell, when it comes in big sunglasses and long hair, that frightens a lot of us over thirty, and worse, fools us into thinking that it's not just a shell at all, but a whole new and

different kind of person in there. And if we hear the shell express some new idea or value—or speak or sing in some strange new language, we strain to hear what was said and try to play back our communication in the same way with the same words. We try, in other words, to communicate with the shell instead of the she or he inside.

He continued:

I can assure you from personal experience that today's young people, however sober, serious, callous, arrogant, flip, or freaked out they might appear on the surface, still cry quietly in the bathroom when a pimple appears at prom time, or when they feel unloved or unsure (which they really do most of the time) or threatened or confused by some of the problems that confront them. I believe that honor and justice and truth and logic mean as much to them as to you and me— maybe more. I believe that beneath the shell, they are simply young people (and it's important to pause between those two words, young and people, to fully grasp what they mean) who, in the main, respond logically to logic, lovingly to love, and honestly to truth.

My parents were hardly saints, and they could also use their words to say cutting and dismissive things. But generally, growing up in their house, the orientation emphasized the importance of grasping the other person's perspective.

My parents' favorite story was one my dad would tell. One morning on vacation in Florida, as he stood on the hotel balcony gazing at the ocean, my dad spotted a young boy walking down the beach alone.

Below my dad on another balcony, another boy, unseen, called out to the boy on the beach. "Jake!"

The boy on the beach looked over briefly, but kept walking.

"Jake!" the boy on the balcony repeated.

But the boy on the beach kept walking.

"Jake! Jake! Jake!" the boy below cried.

Finally, the boy on the beach stopped and turned squarely toward the hotel. He reared back and yelled, "Can't you see I'm some other kid?"

I'm some other kid! I can still hear my dad repeating the line at the top of his lungs, over my mother's roaring laughter.

The communication orientation I grew up with became more like a communication *philosophy* throughout the life I've lived. During a career spent among professional communicators—Chicago journalists, the oral historian Studs Terkel and several of the working-class poets he unleashed, elders of the public relations business, political speechwriters from around the world, and psychologists (including my younger sister)—I've come to see that communication is much more than words.

Communication is pretty much *everything*.

Boe Workman is one of my very best friends in the communication business and a speechwriter trained in classical rhetoric. He writes for the CEO of AARP, as he has for the previous three CEOs of that American institution over the past quarter century. Over cocktails once, Workman told me he had completed an "ethical will"—an essay that would tell his friends and his family someday "what my life was all about." I asked him to share it with me—and after I read it, I begged him to let me share this part with you:

> I am a firm believer in and practitioner of *rhetorical perspective*, having made its study and practice my chosen profession. As a writer, and especially as a speechwriter, I believe in the power of rhetoric to initiate and energize ideas, and in the principle of public discourse to illuminate, refine and resolve public issues.
>
> And as Isocrates wrote in *The Antidosis*:

There is no institution devised by man which the power of speech has not helped us to establish. For this it is which has laid down laws concerning things just and unjust, and things honorable and base; and if it were not for these ordinances we should not be able to live with one another. It is by this also that we confute the bad and extol the good. Through this we educate the ignorant and appraise the wise; for the power to speak well is taken as the surest index of a sound understanding, and discourse which is true and lawful and just is the outward image of a good and faithful soul. . . . [W]e shall find that none of the things that are done with intelligence take place without the help of speech, but that in all our actions as well as in all our thoughts speech is our guide, and it is most employed by those who have the most wisdom.

My Aristotelian belief is that "what makes a man a sophist is not his skill, but his moral purpose," and that in the long run (sometimes a very long run), the worse cannot be made to appear the better reason.

Perhaps that long run has never seemed longer than it does today. But history, too, is long—especially when you start with Aristotle. And human communication is a moral purpose, especially when you do it with more than words.

When you try to do it with your life itself.

Communication Is Everything You Do and Everything You Never Do

I have a theory about communication: everybody already knows everything.

It goes like this: based on the hundreds and thousands of unwitting hints and omissions, odd looks and facial reactions, words and silences, patterns of presence and absence, in person and over text messaging, people come to know everything they need to know about their family, their friends, their colleagues and bosses—about anyone whom they truly care to understand.

That's right, *everything*.

To illustrate my theory, I share the instance that awoke me to it.

Some years ago, a very close family member—someone I have known since we were both small—broke up with a guy she'd been dating for years. I'd always been friendly to the guy—he was boring and self-pitying, but he treated her well and loved her—but I told her I was supportive of the breakup because I thought she could do much better.

"Why didn't you tell me that six months ago?" she said. "I would have broken up with him then!"

And I thought: *You've known me all my life. By now you know what it looks like, what it sounds like, what it feels like when I am talking to someone whom I admire. And you also know what it looks, sounds, and feels like when I'm being polite to someone who bores me, who makes me uncomfortable, who makes me nervous, who makes me sad. I don't need to tell you what I think of your boyfriend; you already know. The only question is whether you're going to acknowledge it, and when.*

So clear was this to me that I began to apply the theory to other situations where people have frequent contact with one another over a period of months or years, and my Everybody-Already-Knows-Everything Theory of Communication began to form.

Because of a thousand wordless signals, a friend knows when he's second fiddle. A sister-in-law knows you like her better than your own brother (and the brother knows it too). A child knows whether or not you meant what you said. A boss knows if you think she's dumb. And eventually, a whole employee population gets a pretty good and common sense of whether the management is in touch with the realities of their work lives, or out.

This is why truly candid communication, when you finally deliver it, is usually not earth-shattering to people who, after all, had more than an inkling in the first place. We have many familiar expressions for this feeling: *The writing was on the wall. I'd known for a while that something wasn't right. The minute she walked in, I knew exactly what she was going to say.*

That's why sincere, sensitive communication—no matter how unpleasant its content—usually comes with an unexpected comfort. It resolves a long tension. It gives permission to acknowledge nagging knowledge. How many times have you heard people say that even something unpleasant—getting fired or their diagnosis or their divorce—came as a relief? Because most often, they knew it all along.

The implication here is *not* that conscious communication is unnecessary, or that it is a mere formality. Instead, it means our essential communication responsibility is not to spoon out information slowly to babies with weak digestion systems. Rather, it's to try desperately to keep up verbally with the massive flow of unvarnished truth that our behavior is unwittingly sending, and that our family, friends, and colleagues are receiving every day. Our words are a constant attempt at reconciliation—or at least an admission of our inconsistency.

Gotta give the guy credit, we so often hear ourselves say. *At least he admits it.*

Or just as often: *I don't mind that she does it. I just wish she would admit it!*

Our words—most of them, anyway—are mere captions to our actions. We can only hope that they describe the action accurately, because we know they won't explain it fully.

And the problem is even tougher than that.

Because it's not so much your regular behavior that communicates most strongly. It's the things you *never* do that say the most.

That's how we sum people up when they're gone, isn't it? Of good people, we say, *She never had an unkind word to say about anybody.* Of bastards, instead it's *He never did anything for anyone but himself.*

How can I most economically tell you about my father? He never got drunk, he never farted in front of us, he never left his bedroom without his shoes on, and he never swore. (Or as my mother, who was a little more salty, told us kids, "Your father wouldn't say 'shit' if he had a mouth full of it.")

It's not what we do that tells the most about us; it's what we *never* do: The neighbors know where they stand, because although you'll play euchre with them, you *never* ask them over to dinner. The CEO has a blog on the company intranet and shows up at all the employee meetings, but she *never* eats in the employee cafeteria.

The parents who get along most of the time but *never* hold hands, or the mother who never said she loved you. The friend who never calls you first, the colleague who never seeks your opinion, the client who never asks how you're doing. Specific and general, these "never" behaviors are the ones that say the most, because they speak the truth far more powerfully than the things we consciously do.

What do *you* never do?

Communicating Is Hard Because Being a Person Is Hard

Sometimes we're reminded, by Facebook posts or by needlepoint pillows, to go easy on other people because you never know what burdens they are carrying. Instead, I try to go gentle on people because I know *exactly* what burdens they are carrying.

To be a fine human being, you have to be . . .

Strong and gentle

Proud and humble

Enthusiastic and calm

Fun and serious

Bold and careful

Self-aware, but not self-conscious

Candid and discreet

Discriminating and democratic

Loyal (when it's called for)

Generous, but not to a fault

Self-loving, but not self-worshiping

Sometimes aggressive, but never violent

Intellectual and instinctive

Logical and musical

And to *raise* a fine human being, you have to teach someone else to be all these things. Yet that's not all—because all those proportions change with time and circumstance and your relation to everyone else in your world.

When I was a teenager, I got in some trouble with alcohol and drugs, and I spent time in a treatment facility. The counselors there were all recovering alcoholics, and some of them didn't seem like they'd been recovering for too long. One particularly red-faced counselor—his name was Tim—didn't like the cut of my jib. He thought I was sarcastic and arrogant. I didn't see myself that way, and I told him so. He pointed a half-amputated index finger at me and yelled, "You need to see yourself as other people see you!"

I've honestly wrestled with that idea for many years (and over many beers). How productive is it, really, to see yourself as other people see you? And which other people should you use in that exercise: the ones who love you, the ones who hate you, the ones who pity you, or the ones who envy you?

I think there's a danger in thinking too much about how other people see you. (And as my father used to helpfully remind his teenage kids, "You'd worry less about what other people thought about you if you realized how seldom they do.")

Yet there is also a real danger in *generally* misinterpreting the way you're seen by other people. Of a man with preening self-regard unshared by others, it used to be cuttingly said, "He was made much of by his mother."

And circumstances change the context. When you were the third-shift foreman at the stamping plant, everyone saw you as a sage, courageous labor voice—but now that you've been retired a few years, suddenly you come across to the very same people as a tiresome Facebook crank. Or you just age out of your charm, unknowingly transitioning from a strong-minded young woman who excites people to a grumpy old lady who embarrasses them.

I once had a conversation with a middle-aged English teacher who was in the process of taking on his third entirely new persona at the school.

When he was in his twenties and early thirties, the seventh-grade students regarded him as a big brother and cooperated with him out of admiration. Then one day when he was in his mid-thirties, he yelled at a class and saw to his surprise that they were terrified. "I realized they related to me as their father now," he said, and he had to modify his approach accordingly. So throughout his forties and early fifties, he behaved as a father.

Then one day—not long before he and I had this conversation—the teacher yelled at a class in his thunderous Dad voice, and detected pity on their faces. *Uh-oh* was how he read their look. *Gramps is losing it.* And so he knew he had to establish a wholly new basis of influence: an elder's role.

We must adjust.

In one way or another—and in many areas of our lives, and often from hour to hour—we all have to play so many roles and contort into various positions. For those who gracefully pull off all those athletic maneuvers, there ought to be a hall of fame. For those who don't—they should be gently coached by the people who love them, because life is hard enough by the day. Keeping up with it by the decade is a hell of a lot to ask of ourselves and of one another.

And most failures, we should forgive.

Ask for What You Want

How to make an apple pie: first, get a stove.

Communication has a similarly overlooked first step: ask for what you want.

I call this the Ron Santo Rule of Communication, and here's why: For many consecutive years, when it came time to choose another group of players to be inducted into the Baseball Hall of Fame, Chicago reporters sought out Ron Santo, a longtime star Cubs third baseman who had become a popular radio announcer for the team. They asked Santo how he was feeling about his chances of getting in. Santo, who had lost both legs to diabetes, more or less cried out in agony every year: He wanted so badly to be voted into the Hall of Fame. He believed he deserved to be in. And he was trying not to get his hopes up for the umpteenth straight year of crushing disappointment.

But every year, he wouldn't get in, and the reporters would drag their cameras back to capture Santo's tears. *Maybe next year . . .* Santo had retired in 1975, and this went on until he died in 2010.

People loved Santo—not *despite* the guileless enthusiasm with which he played and lived, but *because* of it. People like people who ask directly for what they want—partly because we're all surrounded by people who ask for one thing when they really want another, or people who never ask at all but somehow resent us for never giving it to them—and we want to do our best to grant an honestly expressed request.

I was pleased to see that my daughter had figured this out by the time she was in sixth grade.

My wife and I were at her parent-teacher conferences, making the rounds. We had to meet with four teachers—science, social studies, reading, and math—and there was lots of waiting for these brief and shallow encounters. Finally, we'd seen three out of the four teachers. Our daughter had all As. Did we really need to wait around to talk to Mrs. Novak, the math teacher?

"Yes!" our daughter said.

"Why?" we asked, hungry and hot and tired of being there.

"Because she's going to say a bunch of nice things about me," she replied, "and I want you guys to hear it."

"But we already know it."

"Yes, but I want you to hear her say it while I'm sitting there."

"But why?"

"Look, I've worked really hard, and I just want you to listen to my teacher saying good things about me!"

What, pray tell, is the proper retort to that?

The most difficult people we deal with daily are those who either don't know what they want in their life—or even in their Saturday afternoon—or do know but haven't the courage or the confidence to state it plainly. And the sanest, happiest, most agreeable people in the world are the people who do know what they want, and who—in the full understanding that others have desires too—say so.

Ron Santo's sleeve-sewn heart didn't get him into the Hall of Fame during his lifetime (he was inducted posthumously). But it won him the adoration of millions of baseball fans and almost everyone in Chicago—a love that kept him on the radio until the end, despite his rather meager gifts as a baseball announcer.

And yeah, we waited around to hear Mrs. Novak tell us what a delight it was to have our daughter in her class. All on account of the deceptively simple Ron Santo Rule of Communication—ask for what you want.

I hope she never forgets it.

Communication Can Bring Us Together, Even in Mutual Appreciation of How Far We Are Apart

For his motto as a writer, my dad used a Latin phrase meaning "we are all the same." That's what he believed: that people are far more alike than different in the most important ways, and that the purpose of communication was to reveal our essential similarity and thus bridge—or magically erase—a perceived divide.

But sometimes, communication shows a *difference* where we did not believe there was one. And that can be useful too.

One night a few years ago, I found myself in a noisy, crowded bar with a group of people that included a woman I know only a little bit, but whom I like a lot. I see Hillary maybe once a year, always when we've each had a few drinks, and we blast straight into intense talk—about work (she's an interior designer with a lot of absurd ideas, and I'm a writer with some of my own) . . . about the fortunes and character of the friends we have in common . . . and about raising only-child girls. On this night, her daughter was eight years old and mine was soon to be eleven.

Over the pounding music, I leaned into Hillary's ear and downloaded a verbal essay about how raising a kid means gradually realizing that you have not, in fact, created a one-of-a-kind genius-saint who, because of your inspired and meticulous influence, is and will forever be utterly devoted to the very highest things in life, and uninfluenced by the world's grossness and people's stupidity.

As your child grows into herself (I continued at the top of my lungs), you must increasingly acknowledge that you have created a person who, however immaculately gorgeous to you, is actually a lot like the rest of us: muddling along all day, trying to do some damned thing that's useful, and hoping not to act as jerky and selfish and thoughtless as we usually do.

As a loud Ramones tune gave way to an even louder Clash song, I added that when my daughter was born, the Black receptionist at the publisher I worked for declared her belief—offering no evidence except her own tears (and the fact that we named our daughter Scout)—that Scout would become "the next Martin Luther King." I remember having to work hard to pretend to be skeptical. Under my careful direction, *of course* Scout would become the next Martin Luther King. Actually, she would be a guitar-playing, motorcycle-riding Martin Luther King who could dance the tango, tell a good joke, and drink you under the table.

Hillary is a good listener. Also, I was shouting in her ear, so I couldn't really look in her eye until I had concluded my oral argument.

When I finally did look her in the eye, I said expectantly, "You know what I mean?"

And she shouted back with a big smile on her face, "No! Not at all!"

"You mean you never fantasized that your daughter would be a saint and then later had to adjust your expectations, realizing that although they're totally natural and every parent has them, they were in fact asinine?"

"No! I never had those expectations!" Hillary replied. "And it's a good thing! Because my daughter quite often comes home from school knowing she's been a jerk! I never thought she'd be anything other than another imperfect person, just like her father and me!"

She said it all in a way that made me unable to dismiss her denial as some kind of earthy, humble pose. She said it with an open face and a matter-of-fact tone that didn't judge me harshly for what we both suddenly saw as my crazy and entirely egotistical point of view.

We both laughed. It was funny, and now she and I laugh about that conversation every time we're together. I had communicated a deep, closely held idea to a person who I thought was a very like-minded parent of an only-child girl—to a woman of my generation and socioeconomic class and political orientation—with an assumption that *we are all the same.*

I wonder how you say in Latin, *No, we aren't!*

But we are bonded by honest conversation nevertheless.

In Communication,
Your Enemies Are Your Friends

B ouncing through Copenhagen's town square one night, brimming with the euphoria you feel after giving a speech and getting the heck out of there, I heard myself spit out to my Danish host a public-speaking technique that I'd been using all along, though semi-consciously.

I think it contains some broader communication wisdom, too.

At the beginning of every talk I give, I locate one person in the audience—and she's always out there—who appears to agree with everything I say, even before I say it. She's nodding and smiling, laughing and clapping, even when I'm only taking a drink of water. I find her without even thinking about it, and I note her location. She is, and will be for the rest of the speech, *my mom.*

Just as unconsciously and inevitably, I find her opposite: the Resting Bitch Face Dude who loathes me on sight, who has me pegged as a glib, smug hotshot before I even open my mouth. He sits with his arms folded (gee, I wonder if he knows his body language indicates that he's closed off to my message) and makes a point to glance at his watch whenever I catch his glare. And catch it I must, because RBFD must be dealt with too.

For the rest of the speech, when I need a little confidence that at least someone out there loves me, I look at Mom. Worst-case scenario, I catch her with her mind wandering, and she immediately snaps to attention and smiles real big and approving. Her smile says, *You're wonderful.* Thanks, Mom.

At other moments—usually when I'm about to make a real strong point or say something defiant—I look over at RBFD, and I lay it on him straight. Sometimes I win him over, and other times I just realize I've got nothing to fear from the guy but fear itself. I stare him down: *I'm up here, Buster, and you're down there.* Still, RBFD keeps me in line. He makes sure I back up what I say with a little proof.

And really, those are the only two people in the audience who matter. I don't look at anyone else. Occasionally, someone else will laugh particularly hard at something I say, and I'll give them a friendly glance. Or I'll accidentally glimpse an odd look on someone's face. But mostly, it's just my mom and RBFD, RBFD and my mom, from beginning to middle to end.

And in the end, I usually win. Because Mom leads the applause, and RBFD, however grudgingly, is forced by peer pressure to join in. And everybody else in the audience, I have to hope, is somewhere safely in between.

You can't please everybody. And as a speaker, as a writer, as a communicator to any audience larger than one—obviously you need to address your supporters. But it's your skeptics who make you make your message stronger.

When I Get Tired of Listening to the Living, I Talk to the Dead

L ate one night a few years ago, I wrote a note on a scrap of paper and stuffed it in my pocket, and there it stayed—wadded up with my money—until I finally uncrumpled it a week later:

> *Not a curmudgeon, goddamnit. Just not interested in anything that my ancestors didn't experience. Because what's the point?*

I probably wrote the note as a frenzied response to one of the many readers of my communication commentary who used to refer to me, when I was young, as "the youngest curmudgeon in the world." That's because I'm forever naysaying the new-and-improved by tediously pointing out aspects of it that are actually old and derived.

That's fertile ground here in what Studs Terkel called the United States of Alzheimer's, where every new bauble is described as if it were the first bauble ever.

I, on the other hand, gargle old words—saloon, sawbuck, proboscis, palaver!—and walk around my Chicago neighborhood blurring my eyes and trying to imagine what it looked like when my house was built, in 1911. What is the matter with me?

It's not that I dislike new things. It's that my life and work are a continuous attempt at communication not just with the people around me today, but with my dead parents and grandparents—and indeed, with everyone who ever was, and everyone who ever will be.

So a hotel opens on Division Street (once the setting for Nelson Algren's gritty 1949 novel, *The Man with the Golden Arm*), and the twenty-first-century proprietor describes herself as a "beauty & wellness alchemist," and says on the website that her "greatest passion (and challenge) is taking responsibility for my own choices and being aware of the energetic wake I leave for myself, others, and the world. . . . I love to create healing tools which help to unlock intuition and inspire people to stay positive, feel beautiful, and live fully."

Is my instinct to check into the wellness hotel immediately in hopes that I will learn to feel beautiful? No, it's to turn to the bewildered ghost of Algren on the next barstool at the Gold Star tavern next door and compare the racket this dame is running with that of the Algren character who used to run a service on Division Street: finding lost dogs for a fee. How did he know where to find your dog? He was the one who stole it, of course.

When I see an infomercial on the Golf Channel about a new tool that helps you keep your head from moving during your golf swing, my mind races—not forward to the day when the device has shaved strokes off my game, but back to the 1920s magazine ad I once saw for a contraption that tied the golfer's head to a clamp on his testicles. So if the head went up . . .

And in the world of corporate communication, where I work: If you're telling me that some novel concept is suddenly the simultaneous solution to all problems in public relations, marketing, and journalism . . . well, sure—I'll attend the Summit on the Big New Thing. But I'll wear my sepia-toned spectacles to that show and try my best to experience it through the eyes of Nellie Bly, Edward Bernays and David Ogilvy, and P. T. Barnum.

Certainly there are truths and insights that I miss by looking at each new development as something I must explain to every dead person who ever lived. For instance, I wrote some ridiculously reductionist things about the internet when it and I were in our youth, comparing it to tele-phones and the like. The internet went on, without my encouragement, to change our lives in ways that would be hard to explain to other gener-ations. Try describing to a young child a world in which a phone book is useful. It's not easy, but it's fun.

It's just as much fun communicating with the dead about the mod-ern world—and communicating for the dead, with those who live in this world. It's also something close to the meaning of my life.

If You Know How It's Going to Turn Out, It's Not Communication

There is propaganda. There is persuasion. There is publicity. But there is no "strategic communication," despite what so many marketing conference titles promise, any more than there is strategic love.

Someone who would propose to communicate strategically is like the misguided artist described by the writer George Saunders:

> We buy into some version of the intentional fallacy: the notion that art is about having a clear-cut intention and then confidently executing same.
>
> The actual process, in my experience, is much more mysterious and more of a pain in the ass to discuss truthfully.

The idea is ridiculous: that one can flap one's lips (or tap one's computer keys) with an expectation of orderly intent, smooth execution, and a measurable outcome. If communication were anything like that, I reckon I wouldn't be as interested in it as I am—or as afraid of it.

I dread a business cocktail party, even though I'm the extroverted head of a professional communication association. Everyone dreads a business cocktail party; that's why they let you drink. I know an outgoing industry raconteur like me who found himself in a buzzing ballroom and panicked. He answered his wallet and ran out the door, pretending it was an emergency call. It *was* an emergency call.

I dread a lunch with someone I don't know. I usually arrive thirty minutes early: ten to be safe, plus twenty more to psych myself up in the parking lot. And looking at our menus and deciding what we want—this is what Emily Dickinson would call the "Hour of Lead."

I dread almost all telephone conversations. How many times have I readied myself for a big call—even one that could offer a real opportunity if it goes well—and as the phone rings, I find myself hoping Oprah won't pick up after all and I can just go back to my regular day.

That's because I dread communication.

I dread it like I dread a long run in January, because of the energy I know it will demand and the pain it will entail.

I dread it because at least half of it is out of my control, which means all of it is out of my control.

I dread it because it happens so fast, and because it can get out of hand and *it can go all the way bad.*

I dread it because it involves electrical impulses and rhythm and bodily fluids and God knows what else.

I dread it because it is unpredictable—like a *big* argument with your spouse . . . or sex with not-your-spouse . . . or opening the thick envelope . . . or hearing the test results . . . or mysterious feet on the stairs . . . or death itself.

I dread it because it is *communication*—and I *love* it because it is communication. But if it's not a little scary, it's not communication.

And if it is communication, it sure isn't "strategic."

In Communication,
the Style Is Part of the Substance

Early in the Trump administration, Christopher Ruddy, the CEO of the conservative news agency Newsmax Media, wrote in the *New York Times* that President Trump's bluster is purposeful. For example, Trump begins by promising he'll stop allowing China to "rape our country," and eventually China comes around to more strongly supporting our position on North Korea. And so on.

Ruddy, who had been traveling in China and had heard ordinary Chinese people call Trump "strong," concluded:

> [Trump's] theatrical persona, his rallies and his hyperbolic tweets have become the "big stick" he waves from his transformed bully pulpit. . . .
>
> Even I do not agree with everything the president says or does. But we should be willing to recognize that, at times, he can be very effective. The Chinese have.

I considered this point from the other extreme, in an essay I wrote fairly early in the Obama administration about that president's communication philosophy, and why I appreciated it.

> I'm always fielding assaults from my left (and sometimes from myself) saying President Obama is a pussy, a wimp, a

coward, or a bad negotiator—on health care, on gays in the military, on taxes for the rich.

What am I defending? I'm starting to think it's his negotiating style more than his policies.

My oldest and dearest pal is a contractor and a tough negotiator—no doubt about it. I love to listen to him chew people up on the phone. When he haggles, he starts hundreds or thousands of dollars lower than I would have dared. And he asks for neither permission nor forgiveness. If he sees a clause in the contract he didn't agree to, he just crosses the clause out, signs the thing, and faxes it back. It's impressive. He's a good businessman, and he has made a lot of money.

He has seen me negotiate, too. And whether it's for a used car or a book deal, when it's all over, he calls me a "dumbass."

Which stings—I won't kid you. And I used to concede the point. But now I'm not so sure I do.

Here's how I go about getting what I need: I very carefully figure out what I think the job is worth—what it's worth to me, to the employer, and to the market. Usually those are three different numbers, and a compromise must be reached. But I do most of the compromising in my head.

So when it comes time to tell the employer or client what I will and won't work for, I present the number that I really believe makes sense—not an outrageous roundhouse punch that will inevitably be answered angrily by a hard left hook, and then counteroffered back and forth until both sides are left to hold each other up in the center of the ring like punch-drunk boxers.

When I do this my way, over the long haul (and I keep clients over the long haul) the client comes to understand that my initial offer isn't very far from my bottom line. So the counteroffer, if it comes, doesn't come in too low.

I've made a pretty good living as a freelance writer, in some pretty tough economic times and through the journalist's equivalent of the Great Depression. I've certainly left some money on the table, especially on short-term gigs where I might have gouged some clients (a couple of whom probably deserved it). But overall, I think I've gotten fair compensation for my skills and the energy I've given, and I simply don't believe a better negotiating style would have significantly improved my income.

Why do I negotiate in this polite and rational manner? My shrink might have another theory, but here's mine: I don't like seeming unreasonable in negotiations with people who need me to be reasonable once they hire me.

I think that is more or less Obama's theory, too. I'm not sure it's always the right theory—there's a chance that both of us behave the way we do because we're adult children of alcoholics, or something—but I do appreciate how he goes about it.

If he's afraid of something, it's not Republicans. It's being seen by others as unfair or irrational.

Maybe I'm not defending Obama as much as I'm defending myself.

Maybe I should stop.

(But it's in my nature.)

Since I wrote that, I've become a business owner myself—now reconciled to floating or sinking in a roiling revenue stream, with a payroll to meet and loans to pay off and every incentive to take maximum financial advantage in every situation. The week I bought my business, I wrote, "I wonder how my own mind and soul will respond long-term to that straight-up, bottom-line pressure and the direct temptation of greed. I've always been a little disdainful of the hard-charging entrepreneur. Was all that monomaniacal pushiness really necessary? I guess I'm about to find out." And I asked my colleagues and friends and family to keep me honest.

A few years later, I can tell you that a certain type of monomania has indeed been necessary for me to run and build a business. But I don't think the people who work for me or teach for the Professional Speechwriters Association would call me pushy. Essentially and basically, I still think about what's right and reasonable and sustainable for all parties— and that's what I propose. And I think that approach has paid off.

I probably could have driven a few harder bargains in my first year of business. But I might not have such friends and loyal partners now in my fifth year.

I believe this maxim to be true, however imperfectly I have heeded it: If you communicate as if life is essentially a war and a power struggle, then your life will be a war and a power struggle. If you communicate on more peaceful terms and with more gentle words—you have a *chance* for a peaceful and happy existence, surrounded by people who love you and people you love.

"Civility" Is Not Communication

Ever since people found out I was working on a book about how Americans can better communicate with one another, I'm getting lots of suspicious questions, especially from friends who worry that I'm going to become one of these mincing, ineffectual twerps who advocate for "civility."

When I announced the book would be published, a onetime editor of mine emailed to congratulate me, and then wrote: "I'm curious about one thing: Who are the bad guys in your story?"

"We all are" was my answer. "Luckily, we're the good guys, too."

I doubt that satisfied him. Here's what I think I meant:

Yes, it's terrible to be terrible. Internet trolls are terrible. I think Roger Ailes was terrible. Someone else might think George Soros is terrible.

But civility isn't a high virtue either. Civility, all by itself, never achieved one good thing.

Civility is a cold civil war.

Civility is a hiss.

Civility is a cowardly mutter: *I bet you're a racist.*

Civility is staying together for the kids, who are nevertheless suffering from the tension in the house.

Civility is the new "tolerance policy."

Civility is *I think you're an idiot, but I'm not going to tell you.*

Civility is *I think you're an idiot, and I'm not going to tell you—but I will shake my head behind your back. And I will tell the next person I see that you're an idiot. And I will probably tell you, too, when you finally go too far and I've decided enough is enough (or I've had too much to drink).*

Civility is *It's you and people like you who are ruining this country! Excuse me, I meant to say, "Pass the salt."*

Civility all by itself is *I hate you, and I'll never understand you, but I'll put up with you because I should.*

Civil *communication*, on the other hand, is something else entirely.

Civil communication is *I might be wrong. I might be blind in one eye or deaf in one ear. There's something I might be missing.*

Civil communication is *Even though you voted for an idiot, I just saw something in you that I deeply admire.*

We are all brothers and sisters—even the guy I saw on the street the other day, wearing a cowboy hat *and* those weird running shoes with the toes.

I've tried to be less violent and more gentle in my own communication over the past few years. That hasn't come naturally to me, having spent my twenties falling in love with the devastating American social critic H. L. Mencken, who purposely, bombastically, and often hilariously dismissed whole swaths of the country—the South, for example. He strove "to combat, chiefly by ridicule, American piety, stupidity, tinpot morality, cheap chauvinism in all their forms." The purpose of these provocations was often, as Mencken put it, to simply "stir up the animals."

I've also been inspired over the years by gonzo journalist Hunter S. Thompson, who portrayed a nation that was largely populated and ruled by greedy, atavistic monsters, whom he casually dubbed "waterheads" and "pigfuckers."

And my first boss, Larry Ragan, urged us to (judiciously) follow the P. T. Barnum dictate: "If you want to draw a crowd, start a fight." Larry once wrote something in a newsletter that drew angry letters from one-third of his publication's readership.

There have been times in this country when instigation was exactly what the moment called for—but now is not that time. As far as most of us are concerned most of the time, this is a moment when communication is most often needed. The animals are already stirred up. People are going around in T-shirts that say *Land of the Deplorables*. The cable news channels are following P. T. Barnum's philosophy so cleverly that these days even the comfortable are the afflicted. I don't even think Fran Lebowitz is as funny as I used to.

Less and less do I as a writer—or as a colleague, husband, friend, or father—feel that what is needed from me is a rhetorical broadside.

It's not just the times that have changed. As a younger man, I thought of communication as using words to convince others of my point of view, in all of its unique subtlety and wisdom. So I felt obligated (and exhilarated!) to contribute my unique argument to every human tussle I came across, including the ones I started myself. Yet the more I think of communication as the life I live, the less important the words I write and speak seem in proportion to all the things I do, and all the things I never do—in public and in private, too. And the less important my words seem, the easier it is to withhold comment without biting my tongue until it bleeds.

When my wife and teenage daughter read these paragraphs, they will laugh at the difference between the saintly, silent monk who claims to be writing this book and the opinionated, know-it-all serial exaggerator they live with every day. All I can say is that communication as a way of life is a difficult practice, taking place as it does in real time, all of the time, and often in less-than-ideal conditions. And all I can hope is that I am getting better at it—that my actions do less harm and more good, and that my explanations of those actions hold more water.

I laughed grimly when I read in the *New York Times* about the 2015 death of Alfred C. Snider, a revered forensics scholar who saw debate as the way to heal all of our worldly woes. Snider was once quoted in a publication as saying, "My agenda is to fight back the darkness by trying to bring the light of human reason. . . . I want to replace weapons with words." Professor Snider's first marriage, it is worth noting, ended in divorce.

Well, my writer parents' marriage also ended in divorce. And after that, in his late seventies, Dad found a girlfriend. They were fond of each other, but they fought a lot—sometimes bitterly. One night I heard him say quietly as he slipped into his bedroom, and she into hers, "Let's try 'er again tomorrow, Betty."

Communication is *Let's try 'er again tomorrow.*

II.

TALKING HEADS: AN EMPTY LIMOUSINE PULLED UP, AND AMERICA'S LEADERS GOT OUT (AND READ PREPARED REMARKS)

P erhaps living your whole life as one continuous act of constructive communication seems a lot to ask. But for a leader of any consequence and any conscience, a life inseparable from the message it sends should be the most familiar idea in the world.

I'm not talking yet about national political leaders, who exist on a plane of television celebrity. No, I want to begin with the leaders we follow day to day—and the leaders many of us actually are. These are the leaders who hold together the institutions that hold the country together.

If the pastor has a cold, the whole congregation feels a little sick. If the high school principal has a spring in her step, a smile on her face, and a kind word for staff and students alike, a little more learning gets done. I realized in my first supervisory job in my late twenties that if I came to work in a bad mood, it set the tone for the whole editorial staff. Because if the boss was feeling pessimistic or bored, how should the staff feel? (I got out of that job fast, because it made me feel pessimistic and bored.)

What time you arrive at the office, where you park your car in the employee lot, the tone of your voice when you greet the security people, the depth of your daily exchange with the administrative assistant (and everyone else you see in the hallway or the elevator), where you have your lunch, what time you leave to go home, and where that home is located and what it cost—this is the barest list of powerful messages a leader sends every day that have nothing to do with what we consider the "content" of the job. The way the leader actually lives sends its own messages, which either confirm the integrity of what that leader is asking of his or her employees, business partners, donors, or investors—or don't.

When a leader gets up to give a speech—whether at the weekly Walmart stockroom shift meeting or at the World Economic Forum in Davos—the audience wants to be reminded why the leader is up there and they're down here. And they want the answer to be affirmative!

Yep, she's up there because she knows this shit backward and forward.

He's up there because nobody else talks about our mission more clearly and confidently.

She's up there because she thinks about this stuff 24/7, and I don't. More power to her.

What the leader says in that speech—and all the words he or she writes or speaks—matters a great deal. It matters as much as the actual decisions the leader makes. But the impact of those words and decisions is profoundly affected, whether diminished or strengthened, by the extent to which the message seems to emanate from the whole human being.

It has always been thus.

Yet it is far more urgent now—especially in America, where companies and nonprofits are standing astride a nation split in two, and taking fire from all sides in a kind of cultural and political and economic civil war.

Corporate constituencies have always had varied interests. But in the current context, they have dizzying and contradictory claims on corporate loyalty. Groups of employees, investors, suppliers, and customers are not only set against one another but split within, by differing and passionately held attitudes and values that are—in the context of the current political atmosphere—urgently held.

A secular society increasingly distrustful of its own government, and dealing with a press discredited as "fake" by large swaths of the public, is singing (as an old speechwriter put it in a meeting not long ago), "Where have you gone, Joe DiMaggio?"

And to whom is the nation turning its lonely eyes for principled leadership and cultural compass points? With an erratic president and suspected intellectual elite, people need someone to trust—someone to know the responsible, sensible, sustainable "corporate" view on gun control, transgender restrooms, Confederate monuments, immigration, Black Lives Matter, health care reform, tax reform, how to behave during the national anthem, and climate change. And so we are left with (of all people) the leaders of corporations and other large institutions.

What social activists long decried as amoral self-interest in corporations is now treasured as impartial interest in economic and social stability. "Trump can pull out of Paris," said one CEO communication advisor at a conference I attended a few years ago, "but UPS can't."

Corporations and other large institutions, like the military, non-profits, and universities—and even smaller institutions, like municipal government—are now social arbiters by default. And their leaders are being asked for far more than the laser-focused, charismatic workaholism that got the job done in the past.

Are they up to it? They'd better be.

Talking with the Poor,
and Communicating with the Rich

The communication gap between the rich and the poor has been with us as long as the economic gap has. I don't know how to close the economic gap. But I can certainly comment on the communication gap: it is widening just at the moment when the nation needs it to close.

First, let's behold the canyon—not just between the super-rich and powerful on one side and the poor and powerless on the other, but between the well-to-do, educated elite and the working class.

A soccer mom thinks she has a right to regularly and severely berate waiters "because I worked at a restaurant in college."

Well-heeled liberal Chicago parents teach their kids about equality, democracy, and social justice but think nothing of paying extra for "fast lane" passes at amusement parks, because they "can't imagine" waiting in line with everyone else.

Six-figure Facebook friends speak about police brutality as if they know (more or less) what it's like to live and die in an urban ghetto made up of one class and color and policed primarily by people of another.

A new-money relative flies first-class to Europe and jokes about "making everyone in steerage feel as envious as I can by ordering as much food and drink and pillow fluffing as possible."

A derivatives trader walking past a soldier on the street says, warmly and automatically, "Thank you for your service," not in the least bit inhibited by the fact that he knows no more about the size or shape of the soldier's sacrifice than the soldier knows about derivatives.

Seven-figure corporate executives show up for a coat drive every Christmas at an elementary school in one of Chicago's poorest neighborhoods, while the teachers dread the inevitable horde of washed, waxed, and polished execs barging confidently into the building to hand coats to the children. It's a nice thought, as many of the kids do need winter coats. But the execs are overheard referring to "the poor," and one remarks unselfconsciously, "This is the nicest thing I've done all year!"

I don't know many of the truly rich and powerful personally, but I know many of their speechwriters. And speechwriters often talk about their bosses less as colleagues whose ideas they're helping to communicate, and more as exalted celebrities whose suits they are tailoring.

It's not just that the rich are different from you and me. That has always been true. My dad used to tell me how tire mogul Harvey Firestone once refused a Sunday afternoon network slot for the flagging *The Voice of Firestone* variety TV show, angrily bellowing that no one would watch it: "I know what people are doing on Sunday afternoons! They're playing polo!"

But one also hears many more stories of bosses in the previous century who remembered everyone's name, right down to the "boys in the mailroom." Hewlett-Packard founder Dave Packard stood before the company's top managers in 1958 and told them how important it was to "develop genuine interest in people." Why? Because you can't lead people "unless you have a sincere desire to like, respect, and be helpful to others. Conversely, you cannot build genuine interest in people until you have experienced the pleasure of working with them in an atmosphere characterized by mutual liking and respect."

Try to imagine such homely, humanistic thinking coming from the current CEO of Hewlett-Packard or any other organization. You can't.

These days, pretty much all leaders of American institutions—corporations and colleges, nonprofits and federal agencies—are either relatively rich or super-rich. And the rich are more disconnected than ever. My fundraiser sister has observed that the very first thing newly rich people spend their new money on is ways—from gated communities to private airplanes—to avoid contact with the general public.

Many CEOs are so aloof they won't even deign to speak with the people who are hired to write their speeches. Yes, they are terribly busy and their jobs are incredibly demanding—much more so than yours or mine. But really, try to imagine feeling so distant from the hoi polloi that you wouldn't, you couldn't, find thirty minutes to confer with the professional paid to write the words you are going to bore several hundred people with next Thursday evening. Again, you can't.

Here's what speechwriters ought to do with the time they should be spending sharing ideas with the CEO. In fact, here's what all people who help leaders communicate—or all people who exist within shouting distance of leaders—ought to do: They ought to do what the leaders ought to do, what Dave Packard recommended. They ought to cultivate their own genuine interest in people—all over the organization and all around its realm of influence.

If they're going to write speeches for out-of-touch CEOs, they ought to write speeches that are as in touch as possible—seasoned with wisdom, quotes, characters, and stories from the real world. You know, the world that feeds the organization with its employees, its customers, and its social permission to operate.

A professional communicator—typically neither rich nor poor—can choose to be a discouraged and lonely dweller in the ivory tower. Or he or she can seek to know everyone in the organization, learn every interesting thing that's going on, contemplate every impact the organization has on the human beings it presumably exists to serve.

And then the professional communicator can attempt to translate as much of that reality as possible to the bosses. When the chief reads the speech for the first time on the podium, he or she ought to learn something. The chief ought to at least have the haunting sense that interesting things are happening, that there are novel perspectives he or she is not aware of, but should be.

The communicator—and anyone else in and around our large institutions—who merely begins the impossible task of closing the communication gap between rich and poor (and between comfortable and working class) is doing worthwhile work, not only for the organization and its lost-in-the-clouds leaders, but on behalf of our society. Because that society is terribly sick from disconnectedness and distrust—from the kind of ignorance that rhymes with *arrogance* and that fuels so much of the bad feeling that pervades our American discourse.

Authenticity as the New Eloquence

David Kusnet is a onetime chief speechwriter for the Clinton White House. I invited him to speak at a conference of professional speechwriters in 2006—pre-YouTube, pre-Facebook, pre-Twitter. He discussed "the rise of the new media, the death of the common culture, the decline of dialogue and debate, and the growing demand for authenticity."

I could have him back to read the same speech at the next speechwriting conference.

What he was talking about fifteen years ago is what we're talking about right now.

Rise of the New Media

As Kusnet indicated, just as radio and television encouraged leaders like Franklin D. Roosevelt and Ronald Reagan to adopt less formal, more conversational speaking styles, "the cable news networks and the internet . . . are making communications even more instantaneous, individualistic, and informal."

Yes, David, we have noticed that lately.

The Death of the Common Culture

"Americans used to know a few basic texts," Kusnet pointed out. "The Bible, the works of Shakespeare, and the basic documents of our history. It wasn't only the elites. The tribunes of the dispossessed knew that their constituents knew the Old Testament, with its struggles for freedom, and the New Testament, with its promise of redemption."

To prove it, Kusnet quoted speeches from labor leaders that cited Scripture and invited us to "imagine how a presidential candidate would be ridiculed if he or she spoke in as elevated a fashion as the leaders of coal miners and sleeping car porters spoke in the last century." Now, Kusnet continued,

> the only common cultural reference is popular culture— TV, movies, music, and commercials. And so Walter Mondale criticized Gary Hart by quoting an ad for hamburgers—"Where's the beef?" The elder George Bush quoted Clint Eastwood: "Go ahead, make my day." And Arnold Schwarzenegger quotes his own films. And now, in the era of hundreds of cable channels, even the popular culture will not be a common culture for much longer.

At this writing, a Mr. PewDiePie is the most popular YouTuber in the world, with 102 million subscribers. Have you heard of him?

The Decline of Dialogue and Debate

Martin Luther King spoke to white moderates. Reagan spoke to working-class Democrats. Bill Clinton won some of those same Reagan Democrats back, telling them he wanted government to offer "no more something for nothing."

But now, Kusnet said, "it's rare for any segment of society to try to engage its adversaries or even try to speak seriously to the common good. . . . Instead of persuasion, we have assertion."

Authenticity as the New Eloquence

"There is a hunger for public figures like Josiah Bartlett of *The West Wing*, or John McCain in real life," said Kusnet, "whose public voices are distinctive and who sound like they are speaking difficult truths. In a sense, authenticity is the new eloquence."

Kusnet went on to advise professional speechwriters, in light of these four trends, to try harder to capture the speaker's real voice, to grab listeners immediately with bold speech openings, and to "use simple, muscular American English."

"And we can all perform a public service," Kusnet concluded, "by helping public figures give speeches that say what they mean—and say it clearly."

> When you come down to it, that is what our work is all about. Not producing pretty language, or even snappy soundbites, for their own sake. But helping leaders, from every viewpoint and walk of life, find their best voices so that they can participate in the national conversation and advance new ideas which our fellow citizens can evaluate and engage.
>
> If we make that voice conversational and convincing, if we grab listeners' attention early and hold it with the sound of surprise, and if we write American as it is spoken in this century, then we will do our jobs better.

Wisdom ages well.

Communication Is Action!

"You don't earn trust back with one speech," said political consultant David Axelrod after Chicago mayor Rahm Emanuel gave an important speech about police culture in the wake of the Laquan McDonald shooting in 2014. "You earn trust back with actions."

Coming from David Axelrod, that was a lot of baloney.

As an advisor to President Barack Obama, he knows as well as anyone that the right speech *is* an action. Remember "A More Perfect Union," Obama's speech in Philadelphia about race? It singlehandedly defused a crisis just as dangerous to his political career as the Laquan McDonald shooting was to Emanuel's, saving Obama's candidacy by delivering a commentary of such substance that it qualified as an act.

In that speech, Obama shared concrete, as-yet-unheard details from his past, revealing the racial complexity of his upbringing, for which he offered material evidence:

> My white grandmother—a woman who helped raise me, a woman who sacrificed again and again for me, a woman who loves me as much as she loves anything in this world, but a woman who once confessed her fear of Black men who passed her by on the street, and who on more than one occasion has uttered racial or ethnic stereotypes that made me cringe.

And in the course of that speech, he revealed—he *showed*—that he thinks deeper and better and truer on the subject of race in America than any one of his screaming critics. He demonstrated that he understands the problem better than you or you or you. And he offered his own candidacy as an incontrovertible example that progress can be made.

Obama continued:

> The profound mistake of Reverend Wright's sermons is not that he spoke about racism in our society. It's that he spoke as if our society was static; as if no progress had been made; as if this country—a country that has made it possible for one of his own members to run for the highest office in the land and build a coalition of white and Black, Latino and Asian, rich and poor, young and old—is still irrevocably bound to a tragic past. But what we know—what we have seen—is that America can change. That is the true genius of this nation. What we have already achieved gives us hope—the audacity to hope—for what we can and must achieve tomorrow.

And here—with enough sad irony to fill a Russian novel—we consider the political position of Rahm Emanuel, eight racially troubled years later.

In his rhetorical moment of truth, Emanuel offered nothing more than an empty apology. "I'm sorry," he said. For what, exactly? For hiding the tape of the shooting for four hundred days? For lying about not having seen it? For knowing all along that the Laquan McDonald incident was just a glimpse through the basement window of a police department that has been impossibly corrupt since Capone was bootlegging soda pop?

"I take responsibility for what happened because it happened on my watch." Ah, yes—the most disingenuous dodge in the book. When the furnace goes out, does Dad call the family together in the kitchen and take responsibility because the buck stops here? No, because he doesn't feel responsible for the furnace going out—but he does feel responsible for getting it running again. So he swears, he shrugs, and he calls the (fucking) furnace guy.

During his speech, Emanuel pretended he felt responsible, but the family didn't buy it. He screeched and shouted and imitated mammal friends whose voices he has heard crack when they are in distress. But the speech was forgettable and thus regrettable because it offered nothing new—not even new platitudes! "This time it will and must be different," he said. "It will be a bumpy road . . . a painful process . . . a long journey . . ." What—not a *trying time*, an *uphill battle*, a *challenge and an opportunity*?

"This is not the Chicago we love, and this is not the Chicago we know," Emanuel concluded. "This is not the police department we believe in and trust to protect our families and neighborhoods. This is not who we are. And this will not stand."

If a mayor were actually trying to come to new terms, his speech would go something like this instead:

> Like all Chicagoans, I am tempted to say, "This is not the Chicago we know and love. This is not the police department we believe in and trust to protect our families and neighborhoods. This is not who we are." In fact, I was so tempted to believe this that I used every rationale I could find to avoid seeing the Laquan McDonald video—and to keep you from seeing it too.
>
> But now that we all have seen it, I'm afraid we are forced to finally confront the fact that, actually, this *is* the Chicago we say we love. This atrocity and others *have* been committed by the police officers whom we supposedly trust to protect our families and neighborhoods. I know this isn't who we want to be, but today is the time to acknowledge the extent to which this *is* who we are. The question is—and I must answer it, and you must answer it, and we must begin to answer it

today—what are we willing to do to make our city the kind
of place we wish it to be?

That speech, David Axelrod, is how you earn trust back. That commentary would be an action, because it would be a communication—the *act* of one leader attempting to share a novel idea, an acquired insight, a deep commitment in forthright language and the matching physical presence that an audience cannot possibly mistake for "just a speech."

Emanuel didn't show up with a speech like that, because Emanuel isn't a guy like that. It's not the fault of speeches—it's just *that* speech, and the bloodless mayor who delivered it.

The Unbearable Weight of Gravitas

A few years ago, a tech columnist named Rob Walker breezily blew taps for the ancient Roman concept of "gravitas."

"A few months ago, my wife challenged me to name three people in public life today who really have gravitas," he wrote. "Practically the only person we could agree on was Nelson Mandela . . . who promptly died."

(This guy has heady conversations with his wife.)

First of all, gravitas was never a good thing. Second, it's not even close to dead.

Gravitas was always problematic. To the extent that it implied its owner was above the shits and giggles and nervous jiggles of the rest of us, gravitas was a bluff, and a dangerous one at that. It put leaders of institutions—or as Vonnegut rightly called them, "persuasive guessers"—in the position of dads, and it allowed citizens to comfortably revert to their familiar and comfortable role as children. "That's the way it is," Walter Cronkite told us, and we were grateful he didn't send us to bed without dinner.

Gravitas was a guy thing, and good riddance to it. Except that it still is a guy thing, though now it's sometimes employed by women. And just because we don't see it on TV anymore doesn't mean it's gone. Gravitas is alive and well in companies, in universities, and in the military. Do you think people cracked wise with Steve Jobs? Warren Buffett is amiable and good-humored, but does anybody put a whoopie cushion on his chair? As Harvard's president would never say to Yale's president, *hellz to the no.*

We've lost our taste for traditional, stentorian gravitas in popular culture. But we don't live in popular culture, do we? We live at work, and most leaders of the institutions we work for aren't exactly begging us to consider them equals. (Nor do we actually want to see them as equals who just happen to make thirty million dollars a year.) When the CEO shows up, everybody sits up straighter, and any exceptions only prove the rule.

Where gravitas still counts, gravitas is still thriving.

What we need in our institutions and in our culture is something *like* gravitas but more honest—something like the relationship between readers and a newspaper columnist. Indulge me as I move these cobwebs aside.

One of the most wounding things anyone ever said to me came from a publisher on March 28, 2008, a little before noon. Way back in 1992, this guy had hired me just out of college. He and others at his company had trained me—sharpened my pencil, refined my mind, helped form my sensibility—and then promoted me to editor-in-chief of their flagship publication. Eventually I left to freelance, but I remained a lead columnist for a number of their publications.

In the middle of the 2008 recession—not to mention a total change in the publisher's business model, away from print and toward digital— the publisher essentially told me he would no longer pay me for opinion pieces. He would pay me to do heavily reported, fact-oriented, straightforward case studies on the making of successful communication programs, but he would no longer pay me for my columns or my blog posts.

"Dave," he told me in one of those sentences that plays on a continuous loop in the electronic chip on my shoulder, "I can get opinions for free." Meaning, his editors could search the communication-industry blogosphere for posts that communication practitioners and PR people were writing for free . . . and ask those people for permission to repost them on the website.

What hurt me was his implication that the opinions of these theoretical strangers, and their writing, would be just as good as mine—or close enough, anyway.

What made me angry, and determined to this day to prove him wrong, was his lack of understanding of why people read opinion columns in the first place. They don't read them, by and large, looking for new ideas. They usually read them for something like leadership. They want to hear from someone who is anointed an expert—because she's the CEO of Ford Motor Company, because he runs the Red Cross, because she has covered six presidents for the *New York Times*, because he has been writing sensibly and interestingly about communication for a respected publisher for two decades.

Except in situations of extreme uncertainty—invasions, assassinations, epidemics, earthquakes—people don't necessarily want to be told *That's the way it is*. But they do want to be told *That's the way I think it is*, by someone they feel they know, and by someone whom lots of their friends feel they know.

For thirty years, whenever something happened in Chicago, the first question was one word: "*DidjareadRoyko?*"

Not that columnist Mike Royko was infallible or his opinions unassailable—he was a terrible drunk and, increasingly, a bitter man. But he knew Chicago politics and culture as well as anybody and better than most. And we'd known him for all these years. So he was a common frame of reference. His take on a thing gave a community something to agree or disagree with, to begin a conversation that could result in a collective consensus, however uneasy.

That's the kind of gravitas a society needs: honest gravitas, earned by real expertise and reliability over time.

And if we don't have it in popular culture, we'll take it where we can get it: at work, at church, at city hall.

You don't have to be stentorian or aloof or humorless to have honest gravitas. You have to be square with your audience about what your credentials are, what the source of your authority is, and the extent of your claim on the truth. You have to be interesting somehow. And you have to hang around awhile, to prove people can trust you on the subject.

Which means that any one of us could have honest gravitas—and almost all of us *do* have it, in particular stations in our lives.

A shift to a more honest, earned gravitas: It's happening. And it's good. And that's the way I think it is.

If I've Told You a Thousand Times,
I've Told You Once

Leaders grow tired of hearing themselves talk—and of hearing themselves say the same things over and over again. They rack their brains (and their speechwriters' brains) for new themes and messages, on the grounds that *I said that last month*.

But when you remember the lessons your parents taught you, you say, "My mother always said" or "My father always said."

Always.

Not *once*.

Not *twice*.

Not *often*.

Always said.

It's not just what you say. It's what you *always* say.

Leaders should look for new ways to say something truthful—and for new illustrations of its truth.

But don't say you don't want to say it because you've already said it.

If it is important, you must *always* say it.

As you always tell your kids.

Your People Aren't Any More Cowardly and Selfish Than You Are

P   *eople don't like change* is the second most common bromide you'll hear at any gathering of leaders or the consultants they hire. The most common one has its own acronym: WIIFM, as in, *All people care about is What's In It For Me.*

Both statements are dangerous bullshit. Here's why.

"People don't like change."

At its best, a family, a football team, or a corporate procurement department is an infinitely complex social organism that operates, somewhat miraculously, through a group contract with a million clauses concerning goodwill and censure, freedom and limits, helpfulness and neediness, love and hostility, indulgence and duty, candor and lies, experimentation and tradition. These clauses are all honored by winks and nods, shouts and silences, arrival times and departure times, clothing choices and meal choices, strategies made to look like accidents, and accidents perceived as strategies.

Each of these contracts is so vast and multidimensional, and so crucial to the functioning of the organism it governs, that anyone who proposes to amend the agreement without appearing to appreciate its sheer magnitude—or acknowledging the good faith daily shown by every member of the group in honoring it—*must be stopped*. Anyone who tries to adjust the contract must be questioned and cross-examined and, in lieu of an explanation and a full apology for endangering the group, convicted of breach of social contract and punished by immediate removal from any position of power.

It's not that people don't like change. It's that people realize just how truly dangerous change really is to the fine-tuned functioning of the social organisms that give their lives sustenance, safety, and meaning. People demand more than a rational reason to make a change; they demand a leader whom they trust to pull off this difficult trick. Because yes, people would rather die slowly together—which, after all, is what we are all doing anyway—than risk blowing catastrophically apart.

So to leaders who wonder why they can't get people on board for a necessary change: It might not be the change you're proposing that makes people nervous. It might be you who are failing to give them confidence.

"All people care about is WIIFM."

"What's in it for me?" exhales the so-called change consultant, making a ripple on the surface of his martini. "That's all people care about."

This theory groundlessly accuses all humanity of being mindlessly selfish. That's a pretty big claim, especially because it's so frequently made by people making six-, seven-, or eight-figure salaries—about people who are making far less.

Yes, people care about themselves, just like you do.

Also, just like you do, they factor in a number of less selfish things when deciding to read or buy or believe in or vote for a thing. They ask themselves: *How will this affect my family . . . my colleagues . . . my friends . . . my community?* Some of them, when they, too, have a drink in front of them, will even consider their country and the world in their decision making.

Employees are no more change-resistant than their leaders are; and not more self-involved, but if anything, less.

Once Upon a Time . . .
A Story about Rhetorical Pink Slime

O ne of the few downsides of being immersed in rhetorical theory all day, every day, is the amorality of it. It gets on your clothing and threatens to seep through your skin, and you have to wash it off before it contaminates you.

Speechwriters know that audiences are persuaded by various techniques, whether they're employed by defenders of democracy or demagogues—or by demagogues posing as defenders of democracy. And storytelling, over the past decade or two, has been the rhetorical technique du jour.

"As the business world has hurried to get up to speed on storytelling, its advantages over other forms of communication and persuasion have been widely touted," observes business writer Jonathan Gottschall in a piece called "Theranos and the Dark Side of Storytelling" in the *Harvard Business Review*. "But like any powerful tool, humans can wield stories for good or ill. It's time to grapple with the dark side of story."

Google "*Harvard Business Review* storytelling" and on page one you get "Use Storytelling to Explain Your Company's Purpose," "Storytelling That Moves People," "The Irresistible Power of Storytelling as a Strategic Business Tool," "The Art of Purposeful Storytelling," and "Why Your Brain Loves Good Storytelling."

And *now* it's time to grapple with the dark side of story?

As we relearned a few years ago through the collapse of the story-fueled reputation of the med-tech firm Theranos and its CEO, Elizabeth Holmes, storytelling can be used to make a brand—or to make one up.

In America, we've been grappling with the dark side of story from the beginning. Did it make us more cynical about our national roots when we learned that the whole George-Washington-chopping-down-the-cherry-tree-and-confessing-because-he-could-not-tell-a-lie story was made up out of whole cloth? You know, it probably did. When I told my daughter about Santa Claus, she also stopped believing in God because, she said, "I used to talk to God about Santa."

Europeans aren't as enamored of storytelling as a leadership technique as their fun-loving American cousins. They are perhaps sadder and wiser because of a lengthy experience with manipulative, malevolent orators. Or maybe they are just less admiring of hustlers than we are in this country, which hustlers partly built.

European speechwriters I have spoken to have always reacted skeptically to storytelling lectures by me and other Americans. They know our speeches are more entertaining than theirs, and they worry that ours are more persuasive, too. That's why they invite Americans like me to come and teach them these techniques. But they simply cannot stomach the kinds of yarns we recommend that their leaders tell, even when we give them rare examples of their own leaders telling them—like the Dutch minister of defense explaining that he "chose a gun" as his instrument of peace because of a story his father told him when he was young, about his own haunting feeling of impotence in stopping the Germans in World War II.

By and large, Europeans aren't buying storytelling, especially the personal narrative stuff that is fashionable in America (and has become ubiquitous on the TED stage). When I ask them why, they generally describe our storytelling as some combination of boastful, treacly, and dishonest. Their leaders are in place because of their education and their experience and their judgment—not because of some damned thing that happened to them when they were children! I think their point is illustrated in the story President Lyndon Johnson's speechwriter Liz Carpenter used to tell, about handing him a campaign speech that turned on a great Aristotle quote. "Aw hell," Johnson said, marking up the page. "Nobody'll know who the hell Aristotle is." Carpenter thought he was crossing out the quote. But instead he delivered it, changing only the attribution: "As my dear ole daddy used to say . . ."

See, in America we think that's funny! In Europe, not so much. I think it's funny. But I also think the Europeans have a point.

I once attended a storytelling workshop at a large and well-respected company that made medical equipment. As an educational exercise, the storytelling consultant broke the big communication staff into groups and gave them a directive: Make up a story that traced one of the company's products or inventions to a problem faced by a single human being. All sorts of heartwarming tales emerged from the groups about children with cancer and parents coming up with life-saving devices through trial and error.

Moved by the power of it all, one communication staffer asked at the end of the exercise, "Can we do that?"

"Do what?" asked the storytelling consultant.

"Make stuff up!" enthused the staffer.

No, you cannot tell a lie—even in the service of a great story. And yet leaders so commonly do.

A few years ago, I saw a video where a handsome young CEO takes the stage at an employee town hall meeting to introduce the company's new mission. He begins by telling the employees, "So I've been thinking about my favorite memories as a kid."

Because isn't that how everyone goes about announcing a corporate mission statement—by thinking about their childhood memories?

As a kid, the CEO then says, "I would run up this dirt trail to the top of the Berkeley Hills. And when I would get there, I would sit down, and I would stare out at San Francisco. And just looking at the city, it made me feel like anything was possible."

Now, I don't know about you, but when I was a kid and gazed out across vast cityscapes, or even my messy bedroom floor, I didn't think, *Anything is possible.* I wondered what in the world I was supposed to do with all that stuff. But he's a CEO and I'm just a dumb ole writer, so we'll give his inner child the benefit of the doubt.

"So this morning, I put on my running shoes, and ran up to the top of the same dirt trail," he continues, "and I got there and . . . there was a log—the same log that I sat on as a kid."

Amazing! On this very morning of the big new product announcement, the CEO sprinted to the top of the hill and found the old childhood log, and then he ran back down and told his speechwriter in time to get the perfect anecdote loaded into the teleprompter!

"And it reminded me," says the CEO. "It reminded me how I used to dream so much about what my life could look like, and the impact that I could hopefully have on the world."

Spoiler alert: the little shaver would one day decide he could change the world by running a big real estate company. You didn't see that coming, did you? Well, that's because you don't know the handsome CEO. You see, he came to become the CEO of the real estate company—and then he came to embody that real estate company's new mission!—as a result of something even more profound that happened to him as a child:

> Before I share with you [the company's] newly articulated mission, I want to share with you something deeply personal from my own story. I have felt out of place my entire life. I'm the son of an Israeli immigrant mother, and an African American father from Louisiana who left me and my mom when I was just a baby. Through his actions, my dad told me that I don't belong.
>
> When my mom called my grandparents to say that I was born, they—knowing that she dated interracially—asked only one question: "What is he?"

They didn't ask, "Is he happy?"

They didn't ask, "Is he healthy?"

"What is he?"

My mom said, "He is Jewish and Black."

They immediately hung up the phone and disowned us both. To this day and to their death, I never met them; I never spoke to them. They made it clear that I don't belong.

So, thanks to his mother, who told him to dream big and to get a good college education, and to a number of instructive early jobs, the young man found his own personal mission in life: "to help people at pivotal and transformational moments in their lives."

And now that he's the CEO of the real estate company, he wants everyone to have a personal mission. "I want everyone—every agent, every employee, every client we touch—to benefit from the same sense of purpose that I experienced," he says.

OK, but what does this have to do with the deeply personal story about being abandoned by his father and disowned by his maternal grandparents? Well, check out the real estate company's new mission: "Our mission is to help everyone find their place in the world."

Get it? His father and his grandparents made him feel like he didn't belong, but now he runs a real estate company that makes people feel they belong!

"At [the company], we know how transformational it is to open up a door and feel like you're finally home," he continues. "To look out of a window and see a neighborhood that makes you feel like you belong."

There's that word again! It's all about *belonging*—not commissions or interest rates. This gambit reminds me of the old Buddy's Carpet commercials I saw growing up in Ohio. "I don't care about makin' money!" yelled Buddy. "I just love to sell carpet!"

Then the CEO gets solemn:

But too many people need more help finding their place. Every year, forty million people in the United States alone move. . . . Every year, forty million people are searching for their place. . . . At [the company], we're helping everyone find their place in the world. It's incredibly meaningful to me personally that I have finally found my place here, with all of you.

And the crowd went wild. They really did—a standing O. And the video of the employee town hall, posted on the company's YouTube channel, garnered 139,000 views.

And yet we know the speech is utter bunk. Perhaps not factual bunk, but emotional, intellectual, and rhetorical bunk.

This guy's irresponsible father and racist grandparents surely contributed to his identity and may even have given him his drive, but to imply their neglect contributed to the new mission of this company—what hokum. (Imagine the boss thanking the company's market researchers for their report, but telling them he's going with the whole "belonging" theme because his old man flew the coop when he was little.)

That "deeply personal" story he told about his childhood smacks terribly of [insert seemingly searing personal anecdote here]—just something he used to fill in the blank to establish "authenticity." Had the CEO actually been telling employees something private or something truly insightful or strategic about their business, the firm might not have posted the speech externally. But this was just a big marketing smoke ring for everybody to see and to marvel at until it dissipated and disappeared into the spiritual nothingness from which it came.

But really, what's the harm in a little fanciful corporate storytelling, to help everybody feel a little better about the work they do?

No harm done—unless a customer or an employee actually takes the stated soulful depth of the CEO's commitment at face value and tries to hold him and his company to their words—say, during a pandemic-sparked economic downturn.

And what about the next time another leader says she's going to tell a "deeply personal story"? I mean, how many perfectly relevant, eminently relatable stories can one person have waiting in the wings? It won't be long before his audiences start thinking, *Window dressing.*

What really bugs me about this bellyful of rhetorical pink slime—and you can tell it really bugs me—is the distinct possibility that a clever speechwriter wheedled this story out of the CEO and put him up to telling it, on account of "every speech needs a story." Apparently, it's so hard to find powerful, honest stories inside organizations that writers are tempted to go with anything they find—anything they can get the leader to tell.

They should run it by their inner European, whose burdensome virtue is a longer view of history and thus the future, too. As convenient as this story is to tell today, how will its style, substance, and theme hold up five years from now, after two mergers, a layoff, and a public offering? Will the story get a standing O then?

"Three things cannot be long hidden: the sun, the moon, and the truth."

As my dear ole daddy used to say.

Real Leadership

We have a national political landscape that seems, at this point, toxic and confused to almost all Americans. So if you're leading an institution in America—or if you're in any position of influence—you should think of it as leading America itself.

To the people who work at your organization, to the customers who shop there, to the recipients of your service or charity, to the people you partner with—the ethics, the manners, and the quality of your institution's work are the most concrete and relevant manifestation of what this nation is.

American institutions are America itself. And they can be either an example of what many people of all political stripes have come to loathe about the country: elitism and inequality, bad taste and intolerance, materialism and disregard for the individual. Or they can be an island of American decency, pride, and good sense—paying people fairly and treating them like adults, building a sustainable business model, and demonstrating (in deed and word) how they work for the common good.

In other words, organizations can choose to follow the dictates of Business Roundtable's statement on the purpose of the modern corporation, which made much news when it was revised in 2019. Upon releasing the statement, Roundtable chairman Jamie Dimon said, "Major employers are investing in their workers and communities because they know it is the only way to be successful over the long term. These modernized principles reflect the business community's unwavering commitment to continue to push for an economy that serves all Americans."

One hundred and eighty-one CEOs signed the statement. Is their commitment really unwavering? Are those human investments real? Do companies really exist to serve a healthy society?

Americans are starving, *to the point of hallucination,* for a sense that they're united in something good.

The honest question that American leaders have to answer is: Are they?

III.

WHAT OUR LEADERS
NEED FROM US
(HINT: THEY NEED
US TO GROW UP)

Having spoken truth to power, it's time to get our house in order. We the people routinely declare that all politicians are scoundrels. All government employees are bureaucrats. All university professors are arrogant ivory-tower liberals. All military leaders are warmongers and potential war criminals. All CEOs are greed heads, paid the big bucks for their ability to oppress people and pollute the environment simultaneously.

We the people sum up our view by quoting the late comedian George Carlin, about the American ruling class: "It's a big club, and you ain't in it."

It's an adolescent point of view.

I have an adolescent daughter. Adolescents make faces that are unique to adolescents. The eye-roll. The slit-eyed glare. The reptilian forward thrust of the head combined with a canine curling of the upper lip and a guttural growl.

Adolescents slam doors. Storm upstairs. Lock themselves in their room. Pout, until pouting stops working. Then, hyperbolize and generalize: *You never let me do this*, and *All my friends get to do that*, and *I literally have no idea what you're talking about.*

And then, before returning to her room, my adolescent ends her speech with the adolescent's version of *and God bless the United States of America*: "You're such a hypocrite."

What did we expect, during the ten years our children spent gazing up at us like we were omniscient, selfless gods? We never thought to set them straight, yet now we are surprised at their outrage when their growing sense of the world finds us so woefully wanting—so emotionally inconsistent, so self-interested, so limited in our imagination and experience. And yes, such hypocrites. They have found us human.

And I'm afraid that comes as a disappointment so profound, they can't even find words for it. So they snarl, pout, and stomp around for a few years—not until they realize how smart we were all along (as some parents wishfully hope), but until they sit with their disappointment awhile and realize they're not exactly paragons either. Then they remember that they love us anyway and see that we still love them anyway too.

How do I know this is how my daughter feels? Because I was an adolescent once. Still am, sometimes—like when I occasionally listen to George Carlin's stand-up routines. But I find them less funny now, because as comforting as blanket dismissive cynicism can be, it doesn't really work in a democracy. Or as Carlin himself phrased it, "It's bullshit, and it's bad for you."

Because America doesn't need adolescents. It needs grown-ups.

Follow the Leader?

I n 2012, I helped a dying US Army officer write a book about values and leadership, for the children he would soon leave behind. After the book was written but before it was published, the officer's mentor, former four-star general David Petraeus, resigned as CIA director after it was discovered he shared classified documents with his biographer, with whom he was having an affair.

Not for the first time, I had to wrestle with my own conflicting attitudes about leaders, military and otherwise. As did the dying officer. Here's part of what I wrote in *The Atlantic* back then:

> Lt. Col. Mark Weber worked in Iraq for General Petraeus and, like many other Army officers, considered the general a mentor. Weber referred to Petraeus as "one of the smartest and most energetic men I've ever met in my life, which creates a self-imposed demanding nature to the man—I just always wanted to be a better officer when I was around him."
>
> That meant something to me, because Weber is one of the smartest and most energetic men I've ever met in my life.
>
> Despite suffering from sepsis, enduring a surgery, and attending a retirement ceremony presided over by Joint Chiefs Chairman Martin Dempsey, the cancer-riddled Weber cheerfully wrote a book in two months. Along the

way, his editorial proficiency increased at a rate that gave me the uncomfortable sense that my customer was eating the skills I'd been hired for. (I shouldn't have been surprised. Working under Petraeus as an aide de camp for Iraqi Chief of Defense Babakir Zibari, Weber became frustrated using an interpreter and learned Kurdish in three months. Who does that?)

I came to admire Weber very much, and just as Petraeus made him want to be a better officer, Weber makes me want to be a better editor and a more faithful correspondent. But as a citizen in a democracy, I must be able to admire Mark Weber the same way Mark Weber should be able to admire David Petraeus: *wholeheartedly, but without thinking him infallible.*

When we criticize our leaders, we lazily compare them to leaders we perceive as evil—the J. Edgar Hoovers and the Richard Nixons. But most leadership disasters small and large stem from honest mistakes made by honest people with noble intentions but flawed judgment.

People like us.

Take Colin Powell. After he presented bogus evidence for weapons of mass destruction at the United Nations, he suffered the humiliation of his life. But perhaps more of us should have understood and articulated what in hindsight appears to be the plain fact of the matter: *Colin Powell believed what he was saying, but he was wrong.*

Hubris is hardly confined to the top echelons. Weber's memoir is full of his own "failures," as he calls them, squarely. He flunked out of Army Ranger School because of a knee injury he had suffered previously. "I had been dishonest with myself," he writes. "This was a personal and professional embarrassment I could have prevented, but I had allowed pride to blind me." And when he took his first command, it was of an MP platoon whose morale was in the toilet. "If you're looking for a story about a new platoon leader who inherits a mess and turns it all around," Weber writes through still-gritted teeth, "you should skip this section, because it isn't here."

Later in his career, Weber also experienced a series of disorienting successes in the course of a few months: he was chosen from an eligible pool of 37,000 Army officers to win the General Douglas MacArthur Leadership Award, given a prestigious assignment in Washington that included a sabbatical to get a master's degree, and early-promoted to the rank of major. "With all that praise and recognition," Weber admits, "it was difficult keeping perspective."

If our leaders can't assess their own genius and fallibility, clearly, they need our honest help. Or as Weber puts it, "In the final analysis of failure and success, it may be difficult to tell which is which." Even when that kind of perspective is found, I would add, it's easily lost again.

So we must watch all our leaders closely, especially the ones we revere. The more we trust them, the more power they have over us—and the more power they have, the more vigilant we need to be.

The challenge is to keep that balance between reverence and vigilance. The moment a leader reveals his weaknesses, we shouldn't dismiss his strengths. As Weber writes about Petraeus: "Like it or not, he has been a standard bearer for leadership and calm under pressure. So his behavior tarnishes all men and women who seem too good to be true." But we shouldn't let it.

A great nation needs good and great leaders throughout the ranks of its institutions. When leaders do fall for whatever reason, we need others to take their place. And we must remain open to the possibility of greatness in the new man or woman.

> We must each cultivate in ourselves the intellectual rigor
> and the emotional discipline to admire our leaders, watch-
> fully. Perhaps there should be a name for this quality.
>
> I suggest *adulthood.*

Rereading that 2012 piece almost a decade later, it reads more like 1912. Nationally famous figures who are generally admired, as David Petraeus was before his fall from grace, are fewer and further between than they have perhaps ever been in the nation's history.

But I still frequently work with people who serve leaders in the highest reaches of the military, the government, corporations, universities, and huge nonprofits. Some of these people despise their bosses. A few of them adore their bosses. And most of them seek to see their leaders clearly and serve them wisely, helping maximize their strengths and steering them away from situations that emphasize their weaknesses.

Fresh from his CIA ouster, Petraeus read that piece in *The Atlantic* and, through Lt. Col. Weber, called me up. I asked how he was doing. Terrible, he said. Two weeks ago, his schedule had been jammed with important meetings, and he could get any nation's leader on the phone with a few moments' notice.

"And now," I interrupted him, "you're just hoping Dave Murray picks up."

He laughed and asked for my ongoing counsel in helping him return to public life. My counsel wasn't worth very much to him, I'm afraid. I had no magic up my sleeve. But his gratitude for my helping Weber—who lived to see his book crack the *New York Times* Best Seller list—was worth a lot to me. Unbidden, Petraeus volunteered a year later to appear as a speaker at the inaugural World Conference of the Professional Speechwriters Association that I had founded, lending credibility to an institution that needed it.

As only a leader—even an imperfect, tarnished leader—can do.

Speaking Truth to Power: Talking to Myself

Ten years ago, the Murrays got a puppy. I got a lesson in leadership. Charlie was a cute little fellow, a Springer Spaniel.

Yeah, yeah. Within the first week I had spent $1,000 on the dog and on gourmet food, special baggies, potty pads, dubious sprays, and lots of Other Stuff That Dog Owners Didn't Need Until PetSmart Told Them They Needed It.

I had felt the warm ooze of Charlie's shit between my bare toes.

I had mopped up Charlie's piss maybe a dozen times.

Only a dozen, because I'd taken Charlie down three flights of stairs probably sixty times.

I had bellowed *No* several hundred times.

I had lain awake for hours, waiting for Charlie to stop barking from his cage. I can tell you that he barked at the rate of sixty-two times per minute.

Sleep deprived, I had gotten into an email argument with an in-law who felt strongly that I should refer to the cage as a "kennel," because "cage sounds like the zoo." To whom?

I had risen seven mornings before sunup to take Charlie out.

I had had a conversation about buyer's remorse with my wife. Tyrannically but sincerely, I told her that we should ban that sentiment from our minds.

I had missed five workouts, unable to leave Charlie at the house alone yet unwilling to drag him down the sidewalk as I jogged. (They say that's bad for puppies?)

My wife told me I needed to be "strategic" about when I wrestled with Charlie, "so he knows when it's OK to bite." I told her I didn't know what *strategic* meant in this context. She said, "Like, maybe just don't wrestle with him at all."

I had told our six-year-old daughter, for whom we bought the dog, that she mustn't run from Charlie when he nips at her, because he would only chase her more. She continued to run from Charlie every time he nipped at her. "I'm scared!"

Oh, and don't think I don't know you're finding fault with my leadership approach. I use the word *I* too much, and *we* too little. Well, I'm running a three-ring circus here, and I don't have time to play tiddlywinks with everybody's ego.

I had my strategies—for potty training and for less urgent matters of obedience—and stuck to them, and demanded that everyone in the household stick to them. But did I know they would work? No, and so I furtively checked the websites of pet "experts" to see if they had any other strategies that might work better. They didn't.

And I thought: *I think now I know how every leader feels.* Helpless, put-upon, scared—and sorry for himself, with absolutely no moral justification.

Another story comes to mind: I smoked cigarettes until I was in my thirties, and one day I woke up hungover and out of smokes. I fumbled in my closet and found my cleanest dirty shorts. I stumbled down the stairs and ambled down the city sidewalk. It was a terribly bright summer morning, and I squinted and tried to herd random synapses into thoughts.

I took a step and felt a squish under my right foot, and a splatter on my left calf.

I looked down. I had stepped on a baby bird.

I had stepped on a fucking baby bird!

It was dead. There was nothing to do but continue to the gas station, calling myself names: *You big stupid ogre. You feckless oaf. You reckless, addled monster. You drunken, clumsy giant.*

"Yes, give me a pack of Marlboro Lights, please. And a book of matches."

For days and weeks, I told everyone that story, as a sort of serial confession. Everyone told me there was nothing I could have done. It was an accident. A baby bird on a sidewalk was going to die anyway. I probably even spared it an agonizing death.

That, to me, is how powerful people usually do their damage: by accident. And that's how they get over it: quickly, and with reassurance from their powerful friends.

Understanding power requires the same effort as understanding poverty does: empathizing with it in the most personal way we can. One of the few things I wrote in college that I still stand behind is a line in a short story: "All people feel the same things. We just don't feel them at the same time."

People work for powerful people, vote for powerful people, reap the rewards and suffer the consequences of decisions that powerful people make. So, understanding powerful people is a prerequisite for living wisely. And the best way to understand powerful people is to understand how we handle power when we have it—and to admit that we do not always handle it well.

Goddamnit, I said sit!

An Open Letter
to the "Man in the Arena"

I once wrote a pretty devastating magazine profile of a megalomaniacal suburban mayor, and then had the temerity to attend his State of the Village address the next year.

In his speech, the mayor didn't address my article directly—though he had reportedly directed his lieutenants to buy up every copy of the magazine in town so that locals wouldn't see it—but he called me out obliquely by reading a quote from President Theodore Roosevelt's 1910 speech, "Citizenship in a Republic."

> It is not the critic who counts; not the man who points out how the strong man stumbles, or where the doer of deeds could have done them better. The credit belongs to the man who is actually in the arena, whose face is marred by dust and sweat and blood; who strives valiantly; who errs, who comes short again and again, because there is no effort without error and shortcoming; but who does actually strive to do the deeds; who knows great enthusiasms, the great devotions; who spends himself in a worthy cause; who at the best knows in the end the triumph of high achievement, and who at the worst, if he fails, at least fails while daring greatly, so that his place shall never be with those cold and timid souls who neither know victory nor defeat.

Since that amusing day, I've heard a number of leaders—usually beleaguered mayors—use that speech, which is more commonly known as "The Man in the Arena." Do leaders think the audience doesn't notice how self-serving and impossibly condescending such a quote is, coming from a leader?

Dear Arena Man: First of all, you're not Teddy Roosevelt. Neither was Richard Nixon, who also quoted the speech. And neither is Miley Cyrus, who has part of it tattooed on her arm.

More important: We "cold and timid" critics—we journalists, activists, employees, customers, and interested citizens of every stripe—are the ones who notice the dust and sweat and blood on your face, who point out your errors and shortcomings, who decide if your daring has succeeded or failed. And we are the ones, for that matter, who reap the rewards or suffer the consequences.

We "critics" would never declare that society's institutions could run without you. That would be stupid. But worse than stupid is your suggestion that the critic does not count—and thus, that society would be better off without critical citizens.

It's not that a mayor—or a CEO or a president—should avoid discussing the matter of where we all stand vis-à-vis "the arena." This is a terribly important, ongoing conversation in a democracy.

But I prefer to quote from a more obscure writer than Teddy Roosevelt: Larry Ragan, my first professional mentor, at a little newsletter publishing company in Chicago. Larry had thought a lot about insiders and outsiders, and how they relate to one another, and in a Catholic magazine, he wrote a little prayer for them both.

> There are the insiders and the outsiders. Two kinds of people. Two ways of looking at life. Two ways of making things happen.
>
> The outsiders raise hell. They demonstrate; they organize marches. They issue reports that excoriate the establishment, challenge the status quo, appeal to all who thirst for justice.

The insiders? Often dull. The insiders speak a different language: they know the tax tables, the zoning variations, the assessment equalizers, the square-foot cost to educate the kids. You'll find them on the school board, [in] city government, on the village board. Ordinarily not word people, they have mastered the art of the platitude.

Outsiders are often wild. At first, they don't seem to make sense. The first black kids who sat at a lunch counter and refused to move were outsiders. The first marchers to Selma were outsiders. Surely it was an outsider who first proposed the shocking idea that the generic "he" is a sexist word. Dorothy Day, who in the 1950s stopped Manhattan traffic to protest atom bomb tests, was an outsider.

Please God, let us always have outsiders, and give me the grace, in my better moments, to know how to be one. But I'm torn because I want to be an insider too. The insiders resist the first answer that comes to them: they have heard it before. They are offended when they see the world's complexities reduced to slogans shouted into a microphone or preached at a town hall meeting. They are saddened when they hear someone argue that God is on his or her side, and they wonder why God doesn't speak so clearly to them.

Sometimes you've got to feel sorry for the insiders. When they win, few know of their victory. When they go wrong, their mistakes are branded as evil. Often they share the goals of the outsider but continue to say, "Things aren't that simple."

The world is filled with people who like to feel they are right. Insiders are not always certain they are right. They are unhappy when they must resist the simplicities of popular sloganeering. So when we tip our hats to outsiders, as so often we must, let's not do so with such vigor that we fail to give two cheers to the insider.

Isn't that a little closer to what a leader—even a besieged leader—ought to say? And isn't it what the rest of us, occasionally, ought to acknowledge?

Our Leaders Have Plenty to Be Vague About

One of the reasons we don't like listening to leaders is that they're often boring. They prefer platitudes to specifics, banalities to personal opinions, and dullness to daring. They know what they're expected to say, and they usually say it. As a professional speechwriter once put it, leaders need to be convinced "that it's OK to be interesting."

But leaders have very good reasons for their bias toward blandness. Millions and billions of reasons.

The magazine I publish, called *Vital Speeches of the Day*, is a monthly collection of contemporary speeches that has been in print since 1934. Occasionally, I'll dip into an old issue and read it cover to cover. Often what strikes me is that the ideas that are most clearly and memorably expressed are also, in hindsight, the most laughable.

Let's look at the *Vital Speeches* issue dated March 1, 1941. In a speech on railroad regulation, the president of the Pennsylvania Railroad Company complained about people who complain about businesspeople. "If one observes the undercurrents in political and social life of today," M. W. Clement intoned before members of the Pittsburgh Traffic Club, "it will be found that they deal with certain conceptions which are loosely expressed by catch phrases which 'label' them, and which people often do not analyze: such as 'power' and 'wealth'; men who 'run' America; men who 'control' industry; men who 'control' wealth . . ."

Perhaps it was for this speech that "air quotes" were invented?

Most of the speeches in the issue, not surprisingly, debated whether or when the United States should enter what was then referred to as "the war in Europe." Even with Hitler on the march and England on the ropes, the majority of the speeches argued against US involvement.

"They have been fighting in Europe for two thousand years or more," said Senator Arthur Capper of Kansas in a radio address, "and probably they will fight for the next ten thousand years, for that is their philosophy—fighting is their philosophy."

Though that sounds remarkably familiar to the rhetorical carpet bombing some of our politicians lay on the Middle East today, the sentiment is less embarrassing than the well-articulated argument for staying out of the war by Robert Maynard Hutchins, the young and powerful president of the University of Chicago.

"We Are Drifting into Suicide" was the title of Hutchins's speech, also delivered over radio, on January 23, 1941. His central argument was that the United States did not have democracy down well enough to go imposing it on other nations by intervening in the war. Hutchins listed human rights violations and democratic imperfections in America that "leave us a good deal short of that level of excellence which entitles us to convert the world by force of arms. . . . We Americans have hardly begun to understand and practice the ideals that we are urged to force on others."

Hutchins called for a "new moral order in America," concluded that refining American democracy was the first order of business, and warned that the people calling for European intervention were

> turning aside the true path to freedom because it is easier to blame Hitler for our troubles than to fight for democracy at home. As Hitler made the Jews his scapegoat, so we are making Hitler ours. But Hitler did not spring full-armed from the brow of Satan. He sprang from the materialism and

paganism of our times. In the long run we can beat what Hitler stands for only by beating the materialism and paganism
that produced him.

What a magnificent load of imaginatively conceived, authoritatively
expressed, sharply written poppycock!

Just like the leaders of yesteryear, today's leaders are in grave danger
of saying such ridiculous stuff. By virtue of their rank in society and the
interests that surround them, our leaders are encouraged by their boards,
their investors, and their campaign contributors to hold some seriously
peculiar and sometimes borderline insane positions on things. Positions
that, if starkly expressed, might reveal the difference between actual service to the really urgent causes of our time, and that of the lip variety.

And that's often why our leaders don't want to say anything. Because
they'd rather say nothing than say these absurd things. They'd rather
play rhetorical rope-a-dope—and sensibly so—than lash out madly in
defense of the status quo.

My dad used to say old people are quieter than young people, "because
old people have more to be quiet about."

That's true of leaders, too.

We Deserve Leaders
Who Act Like They Like Us

Why did people look so happy at Donald Trump's rallies? Partly because nobody, at a Trump rally, looked happier than Trump himself. And looking happy is a big part of a leader's job.

Rahm Emanuel was the mayor in Chicago for two terms. Nobody ever liked him.

Yes, we elected him and reelected him. And we might have reelected him again had he chosen to run for a third term. That's because he is slick and well-backed by corporate interests. We are afraid of crossing slick, corporate-backed dudes. We have this funny feeling that if we reject them, they'll pull their slick corporate money out of our town, and everything will immediately rust out and fall apart and our property values will go down and we'll spend the rest of our miserable lives staggering around in burlap smocks, like they do in Buffalo.

But it really is true that no one in Chicago liked Rahm. At least, I never spoke with a single Chicagoan who said, "I like Rahm!" And though Rahm's predecessor, Richard M. Daley, had many critics, some of them vociferous and most of them justified, you heard *lots* of people exclaim—sometimes in an apologetic, confessional way—"You know, I *love* Mayor Daley!"

Why did no one like Rahm Emanuel?

The great rhetoric professor Jerry Tarver used to talk about a civic leader who was "so pompous that he could say 'good morning,' and it seemed as if he was taking credit for it."

Rahm had a healthy self-regard, all right, but that was not *quite* the problem with him. The problem was that at every public appearance, he seemed inconvenienced, pained, delayed from the real work of being mayor. Always having to repeat himself. Impatient with the dumb questions. It seemed he regarded us with disdain. He talked to his constituents as if he'd caught a pair of not very bright eight-year-old boys fighting in the dirt and pulled us apart by our hair. And now it was time for a lecture: *I'm trying to be as patient as I can . . .*

And we wanted to say to Rahm (and to President Obama, on whose nerves we also seemed to be occasionally dancing): *We know the job is frustrating, but you begged and begged and begged and begged us for it. So we gave it to you. And now you own it. Can't you manage to appear grateful and happy and game, at least some of the time?*

It sort of seems like the least an elected official could do.

"Because They Know, They Understand"

Did you know there are people who are paid to help the people you work for communicate with you, and to help you communicate with them?

These people are called "internal communications executives" or "employee communication professionals," and depending on how you look at it, they're either not paid enough or paid far too much. But employee communication wasn't always such a fallow field full of HR twerps and vapid corporate PR "people." (Oh yes, come to think of it, you do know them!)

In what may be the unlikeliest opinion you'll read in this book, I believe that a wholesale rethinking (and restaffing) of this obscure discipline could help make America dramatically a better place to work in, and thus to live in, too.

It's also possible that I'm crazy.

Here's where I'm coming from: I majored in English. The year I graduated, the market for poetry was pretty lousy. I tried to get into advertising, but the competition was fierce, and I didn't have the heart for it. I applied for work as an editorial assistant at *Bowlers Journal International* magazine, and it came down to me and one other candidate. He had more experience than I did—as a bowler.

So I answered a blind ad and went down and interviewed at this nutty little company called Ragan Communications that published newsletters for people who . . . wrote newsletters. We're talking about employee communication people who wrote newsletters telling employees what was happening in the organization.

I didn't even know there were such people.

It was a bit of a comedown from T. S. Eliot. But since they were paying $17,500 a year, I took it.

And then I started reading things written by the founder, Larry Ragan. He was a good writer. He made employee communication seem interesting—a series of subtle, strategic battles between democracy and autocracy, courage and fear, permission and forgiveness, idealism and realism.

Employee communication was easy to study back then, too, because it existed largely in employee publications—internal newsletters, newspapers, magazines—and we had stacks of them in the office. In those publications, you could see employee communication people taking big chances with candid stories, controversial letter-to-the-editor sections, and bold headlines like one I saw on the cover of a utility's magazine: "Bad Morale: Whose Fault Is It?"

The employee communicators in those days were ex-journalists who had traded their Woodward-and-Bernstein dream for a fatter paycheck and regular hours. But they were still journalists, and they were trying to ply their old trade from within organizations instead of from without.

Their instincts were mostly good. While mainstream journalists strove to make the world comprehensible for citizens and to give voice to the voiceless, these employee publication editors did much the same thing inside the social microcosm of an organization.

You can say these people were misguided—just wanting to keep practicing journalism, but for a bigger salary—but they were right to see organizations as social institutions.

"Each organization has its own government, religion, education, economy, and family," wrote employee communication executive Ron Shewchuk, an early influence of mine. "Many corporate leaders ignore this and think of their businesses more like a plow that can be endlessly dragged through the ground rather than a society that needs to be nurtured and maintained."

If those communicators from twenty-five years ago did nothing else, they had this mission, whether management shared it or not: to nurture that corporate culture.

That was a long time ago. And I hate to tell you this, but in order to start talking about the future, I'm going to have to go back even further into the past—way, way back, before the 1980s and 1970s, before the 1960s, back down through the 1950s—all the way back to 1942, the year the first-ever book on employee communication was published.

Written by a long-dead corporate employee relations executive named Alexander Heron, the book is simply called *Sharing Information with Employees*, and the employee communication philosophy it articulates is just as plain as the title.

Heron begins his book by alerting us to a quietly radical notion in a world of employee communication people and human resources people who spend their heart's blood trying to get employees "engaged" in the work of the organization. Heron sees "engagement" as the natural response of a human being in a collaborative effort, rather than one more thing to be somehow wrung out of a worker.

He paints what he calls "an image that will remain with us throughout our troubled study of the misunderstanding in industry today."

> It's a picture of the workforce before the Industrial Revolution. It's a picture of a fully engaged workplace.
>
> We might find our picture of the old understanding in a wagon shop, a grist mill, a cotton mill, a pottery or cutlery shop. Let us find it in a furniture shop. Perhaps eight men work there. One of them is the boss. He owns the shop, but he works there, visibly. The other seven receive wages. The work done by the boss is not all done with tools; sometimes

he uses a pencil. He draws designs, writes occasional letters, puts down figures about wages, costs, and prices.

The other seven know, quite closely, how much money the boss had saved up from his earnings as a journeyman before he started in business for himself—in other words, how much "capital" he had and how long it took him to save it up.

The shop or factory is on the same lot as the house where the boss lives; he owns it. The other seven know how much his taxes are each year. They helped to build the ten-by-thirty addition to the shop last year, and they know how much that cost. They were all in on the discussion before the new lathe was bought, and they remember the price and the freight. They remember how the boss borrowed some of the money from his wife's sister.

They know that the dining room "suit" on which they are working now is for Jane Winton, [who] used to be Jane Carey, the schoolteacher, before she married Bill Winton, the banker. They know it has to be as good as the furniture she saw in Buffalo, and that if it is good, Bill's mother is going to give the boss an order for another lot which will keep them all busy through the winter.

They see the finished job emerging under their skilled hands, day by day. They know how difficult it was to get the seasoned walnut, and what it finally cost, what price is to be paid for the finished job, how much the boss will "make" on it, and how much of that will go to pay off the loan from the sister-in-law.

They know that the boss has gradually built a reputation for honest quality and skilled workmanship and that they are part of that reputation. They know why once in a while they have had to wait a little for their wages—when the taxes had to be paid before the money came in for the new counter and fixtures at the drugstore.

Above all, they know the boss. Their attachment to him is basically not sentimental but practical. He is the salesman who gets the orders which bring work to them. He collects the money which pays their wages. He manages to accumulate the working space and the equipment. They are realistic enough to know that they can get their full and fair share of the income of the business. They laugh at anyone who talks of the conflict between labor and capital, between them and the boss.

They know. Because they know, they understand. And in that full and simple understanding, they "put themselves" into every job.

Heron understands that corporations are not furniture shops. But he argues that, to whatever extent possible, they must be made to feel like the shop he describes. Employees need an understanding of the basic economics of their business, who the customers are, who the competition is, what the expectation of quality is, and what kind of person the boss is.

That is the job of the employee communication professional—and ultimately, the job of the leader of the organization he or she serves. With so many employees and such complex organizations, it's a big, tough, endless job. And those who are tiring of it or failing at it often dismiss employees as just wanting to get through their workday so they can collect their paychecks and go home.

Alexander Heron heard that talk from his own peers. And he didn't like it.

They say that some people are just born that way, and they will go on to imply that this is in accordance with some divine plan. It seems to them inevitable that human society be classified and stratified, in the same manner as a hive of bees: If all bees were workers, there would be no organization under qualified leadership. If all were queens, there would be no honey. If all human beings were endowed by nature with keen, alert, understanding minds, none of us would be satisfied to work for wages or at manual tasks; we would all want to be bosses.

This attitude has a lot of history behind it. It is the idea of both ancient and modern tyrannies under which conquered enemies became the slaves of the conquerors.

That's pretty strong stuff—maybe even a little hyperbolic. But what underlies his rejection of the worker bee analogy is the commonsensical notion that a democratic society in a capitalist economy relies utterly on an informed populace. And, as Heron writes, a huge part of an informed populace is an informed workforce:

The deliberate effort to share business information with the great majority who work for wages corresponds closely to the deliberate plan to make education freely available to the people. . . .

[W]e have all of us, every adult citizen, been jointly and equally entrusted with the government of our nation, state, and city. That government is increasingly engaged in the protection and regulation of the economic interests of all of us. It is inconceivable that the . . . millions of us who work for wages can do a good job, or even a safe job, of governing by votes, without knowing more and more about our economic interests.

The American idea has no place for a class predestined to be wage earners incapable of understanding a world beyond the workbench, no place for a class which is denied the opportunity to reason its conclusions on facts which it helps to create, no place for a class which is happier because ignorant of anything beyond the daily task. And those whose sense of superiority leads them to believe in either the necessity or the desirability of such classes are themselves enemies of the American idea or ignorant of its genius.

Do you hear what he's saying here? He's saying that employee communication, robustly pursued, is as important to democracy as public education.

I know it sounds big. I know it sounds heavy—but how can we argue with it?

Toward the end of his book, Heron talks about what real employee communication can accomplish:

If our program of sharing information with employees, through all the channels and methods named above, is completely successful, the result—and the evidence of success—will be questions!

The supplement we must provide is an adequate plan for meeting these questions. Meeting them does not mean parrying them; it means answering them.

Some of the questions will be annoying or embarrassing. Some of these will drive us, the employers, into fields of thought which we have avoided. Some of them will test the completeness of our willingness to share information with employees; they will force us to ask ourselves if we have really meant it.

But if employee communicators succeed, Heron wrote almost eighty years ago, they will have achieved something great.

Without destroying the efficiency of modern big business, the pooling of capital, the productiveness of great industrial plants, we shall have restored the living, understanding relationship . . . into which our grandfathers put their strength and interest, because they knew, and understood!

In other words, employee communication can do great things—for the company, for employees, for society—and the world!

As Heron knew, skeptical employees and union rules make such communication difficult. Reluctant institutional leaders make it difficult. *People* make it difficult. But if we begin to see unifying and democratizing American workplaces as the first-best way to unify and democratize the nation, we might find the effort to understand worth the work involved.

Civics Is as Civics Does

"They don't teach civics in the schools anymore!" cry sensible American old farts of every political stripe.

Until that unlikely day when schools resume teaching civics to our satisfaction, Americans need to practice the civics we want to see in the world—in our own realms of influence—asking more of our leaders and also demanding more of ourselves—at school, at work, in line at the post office!

If you don't know what I mean, it is not as difficult as you think, and it is more rewarding than you know. And it doesn't mean carrying signs or knocking on doors on behalf of political candidates.

I've led a quixotic campaign to save a homely but historically significant Chicago house from the wrecking ball. I didn't save the house, but I helped create a community of history-minded Chicagoans that remains part of my life twenty years later.

I participated in another effort, to get Chicago's public TV station to create more local content. In the process, we had our messages heard and we made lasting community connections.

And just as I was editing this book, the Chicago Park District tried in what seemed an underhanded way to eliminate a tennis league that I've played in and loved for years. I happened to be at a terribly busy time in my life, and I had no time to launch a full protest. Yet in less than four hours of my time over a few days, I had spoken with the proper Park District manager on the phone and satisfied myself that they weren't playing fair, acquired the email addresses of a couple dozen other equally dismayed league players, sent a letter of protest with their signatures—and when that didn't elicit a satisfactory response, walked into the Park District supervisor's office for what turned out to be an enlightening conversation that convinced me the Park District wasn't going to restore the league. But I had built a little political coalition! And after another couple hours of research and conversation, I set up a visit by my tennis-crazed crew to a huge new tennis facility on the South Side of Chicago, eager for more players. And so we left the Park District and have happily formed a league of our own.

And of course, my teenage daughter was around to see it all go down in real time, which is at least as good as any civics class I ever took in school, don't you agree?

Such exercises—and the surprising ease and even the fun of them—remind me not to think of myself the way Wolf Blitzer or Sean Hannity do: as a powerless little fellow watching endless debates from his couch and waiting for my chance to cast my wee vote in the next presidential election. That's not me. Don't let it be you.

Of course, there *is* still electoral politics, and the seemingly ever-escalating *Sturm und Drang* that oversalts our Thanksgiving dinners and sounds for all the world like a nation cracking in half. And we can each participate in that process, too—more responsibly and constructively and powerfully than we currently do.

IV.

WE, CITIZEN: AMERICAN PATRIOTS DON'T CALL THEIR FELLOW AMERICANS NASTY NAMES

Politics has never been my best subject, probably because I did not grow up in a home where politics was frequently discussed.

My father was a bland conservative, and my mother was an ardent liberal. He preferred not to discuss politics at all, and he preferred other people who felt the same way. She was more politically minded, but aside from an occasional exasperated outburst—"You voted for Jerry Fucking Ford?"—she was resigned to canceling out my father's vote in every election and saving her influence for issues closer to home. As for myself, I don't think I knew whether I was a Democrat or a Republican until I graduated from college and moved to Chicago, where Republicans are not allowed.

Many Americans, it seems to me—most Americans, probably—used to feel pretty disconnected from politics. When I was young, we knew some odd folks who were super well versed on the goings-on in Washington, DC—that is, they knew how to find C-Span on the remote. We playfully called them "political junkies," and they bashfully called themselves "political nerds." They were hobbyists of a kind, sort of like ham radio operators or stamp collectors.

These days, all Americans are political junkies. (And perhaps not coincidentally, ham radio and stamp collecting are way down.)

But while we're all political junkies, we're not political scientists, really. We're more like political gossips.

We're variably educated Americans with day jobs and kids and a million other personal interests and personal problems, and a few strong opinions based on some searing experiences—and a strong sense that we should be paying attention at this moment in American history and having our voices heard. Because increasingly since Watergate, few of us feel we can afford to trust the adults in Washington.

So how do we each find ways to speak constructively on American government policy when we don't really have a deep background in it?

I've been working harder and harder on that over the past decade or so, trying to apply what I know deeply—both my personal experience and my professional study—to our disorienting political landscape. And as I've asked myself, I think we should each ask ourselves:

How can we do less harm with our speech—and more good?

Other Life, Not So Far Away

A very good writer who grew up in a small town in Illinois and now works in the city wrote a really thoughtful essay in the run-up to the 2016 presidential election about why the people who go for Trump go for Trump. I haven't read anything better since. "I was born and raised in Trump country," David Wong wrote. "My family are Trump people. If I hadn't moved away and gotten this ridiculous job, I'd be voting for him. I know I would."

I felt I had just enough authority to comment on the piece because I ride my motorcycle on backroads across the rural counties in Illinois, and you don't. On Labor Day weekend in 2015, I took Ogden Road out of Chicago and drove it on a southwest diagonal through many of these counties down to the Mississippi River. I recorded a little of what I saw and experienced on the way there and back. Reading Wong's piece, excerpted several times below, I felt like I was back on Route 34, riding through a world of silent resentment.

Every TV show is about LA or New York, maybe with some Chicago or Baltimore thrown in. When they did make a show about us, we were jokes—either wide-eyed, naive fluffballs (*Parks and Recreation*, and before that, *Newhart*) or filthy murderous mutants (*True Detective*, and before that, *Deliverance*). You could feel the arrogance from hundreds of miles away. . . .

To those ignored, suffering people, Donald Trump is a brick chucked through the window of the elites. "Are you assholes listening now?"

———

Urban sprawl turns into rural road in Oswego—you feel it. And you could probably get a good country breakfast at Plano, Sandwich, or Somanauk, but I didn't take any chances. I waited until I hit Mendota, about a hundred miles west.

After hurtling face-first through the wind for a couple of hours, I walked into Ziggie's Family Restaurant in a zombie state familiar to me from lots of backroad rides through America and Canada (my Triumph passed 20,000 miles on this trip). I tried to appear as a normal human being despite the intense introversion that two hours of engine meditation creates. Tried to appear as a normal American through the protective shell you build to keep Chicago out. Tried not to rub my helmet-itchy scalp while ordering my eggs.

Six old guys sat at the next table over, theorizing about why a tractor axle had broken one day and not another day, talking about a record flathead catch (eighty-one pounds, and the guy threw it back!), and debating with some humor and at great length the proper size of a regulation corn dog, thus to determine what constitutes the "jumbo corn dog" advertised on the Ziggie's menu.

The waitress finally gave in to her curiosity about the spaced-out drifter at the counter, and she asked me where I'd come from. When I said Chicago, she said her sister had dated a fellow in Chicago once.

"Chicago's not so bad," she said, provided you learn a few tricks about city life. For instance, she learned the hard way never to give homeless people money. Because if you give money to one, they'll gather around you by the dozens. "Give them toothpaste or soap," she said. "Anything but money!"

———

The foundation upon which America was undeniably built—family, faith, and hard work—had been deemed unfashionable and small-minded. Those snooty elites up in their ivory tower laughed as they kicked away that foundation, and then wrote 10,000-word think pieces blaming the builders for the ensuing collapse.

———

The next stretch is farm fields punctuated by happy speed reductions into towns so small—Dover, Princeton, Wyanet, Sheffield, Neponset—that when you hit Kewanee (pop. 12,676), it feels like a metropolis. After that, you're glad to get back out to the country, and to Galva (pop. 2,758) and then Altona (pop. 531) and Oneida (pop. 700).

I stopped and listened to the Altona Tigers marching band, rehearsing out of their uniforms; they didn't sound good, but they sounded wonderful. I think it was also in Altona that I took a photo of a Lutheran church sign: *Worrying is like praying for what you don't want!*

———

The rural folk with the Trump signs in their yards say their way of life is dying, and you smirk and say what they really mean is that Blacks and gays are finally getting equal rights and they hate it. But I'm telling you, they say their way of life is dying because their way of life is dying. It's not their imagination.

―――――

On the return trip: the utter stillness of Labor Day in the country. I rode through many towns without seeing a soul; I was looking for a tavern for lunch, but even most of those were closed. I resigned myself to wait until I got to the big city in Kewanee, where they'd just be wrapping up their annual Hog Days festival and some places would have to be open. But then I spotted Mary's Restaurant, on the eastern outskirts of Galva. There were a few cars outside.

Eight locals and a middle-aged biker couple nursed beers in dim light. The kitchen wasn't open, so the only food available was chicken soup and chili, simmering in crock pots. Six dollars, all you could eat, out of Styrofoam bowls. And so utterly homemade, passing it up would have been like snubbing your grandmother.

The Cubs played the Cardinals on the TV. It emerged that half the crowd were Cubs fans, half Cardinals. The Cubs were winning, but the Cubs fans knew this was the Cardinals' year, and so did the Cardinals fans.

"You must be Mary," one of the bikers said to the woman behind the bar.

"Who else works on holidays?" Mary asked, rhetorically.

―――――

So yes, they vote for the guy promising to put things back the way they were, the guy who'd be a wake-up call to the blue islands. They voted for the brick through the window. It was a vote of desperation.

―――――

I pulled off to look at the Hennepin Canal. A little later, I rode past a No Trespassing sign, a quarter mile down a narrow path through a soybean field to the base of a wind turbine, for a picture. I rode through the parking lot of a rollicking biker bar in a grain mill near Langley but didn't stop for a beer because I wasn't feeling bold enough to walk alone into a place called Psycho Silo.

In the next town I saw another church sign—someone ought to collect these messages in a coffee table book—that said: *Living without God is like dribbling a football.*

And I rode to the back of a cemetery at Wyanet and lay down in the grass for a nap. Though I was exhausted, unseen insects tickled my arms and neck each time I started to drift off.

———

"But Trump is objectively a piece of shit!" you say. "He insults people, he objectifies women, and cheats whenever possible! And he's not an everyman; he's a smarmy, arrogant billionaire!"

You've never rooted for somebody like that? Someone powerful who gives your enemies the insults they deserve? Somebody with big fun appetites who screws up just enough to make them relatable?

———

I sat at a hundred red lights, burning from above in the ninety-degree late-afternoon sun and baking from below from the heat of my own engine, as Route 34 turned back into Ogden and a record-long strip mall and then into the city. A family of eight Black sisters almost got killed running across Cicero, and cops ran a red light just because it was the ghetto, and I almost crashed my bike trying to get a stupid video shot of the approaching skyline as I emerged from the bridge at Ogden and Western.

It didn't seem like Labor Day in the city. It didn't seem like any holiday at all. Who works on holidays? Mary in Galva, insects in Wyanet, and all Chicagoans, just to survive.

What kind of a life is this? It's a rigorous life, at least. It's my life, for sure. It's important to know there is also other life, not so far away—and it's important to see that other life as clearly as I can, to the extent I can will myself to slow down and look . . . to make eye contact and see . . . to calm down and listen.

We'd Get Along Better if
We Listened Better—to Ourselves

A funny, brilliant, musical, conservative speechwriter friend told me he was deeply upset by a *Huffington Post* column that basically claimed conservatives are dumber than liberals. As a liberal, I found the article's suggestion that there is a physiological difference between liberals and conservatives less offensive than absurd.

Here's what I think about liberals and conservatives: yes.

Every sane human being has conservative instincts and liberal ones. We each have an inner looker and an inner leaper, a miser and a spendthrift, a lover and a fighter, a hunter and a gatherer. We've each had experiences that led us to trust institutions, and we've had experiences that warned us not to. We've been rebels, and we've been team players. We are strict disciplinarians overcompensating for our permissive side. We've given, and we've kept for ourselves.

It's not that there are two kinds of people in the world; there are two kinds of people in ourselves.

In this infinite world, none of us has either the stamina or the time to thoroughly think and feel our way through every issue that comes down the pike. How many topics do you truly feel ownership of because you've put in the person-hours studying them from every angle? One? Two? Maybe three? And I bet you don't favor universally "liberal" or "conservative" solutions to those issues, but rather some combination of both.

Yet because we are unable to wonk out truly independent stances on healthcarereformdefensespendingabortionstemcellresearchglobalwarm-ingguncontroltaxreformMiddleEastpolicy, we eventually pick one of the two groups to associate with most of the time. When in doubt—and we're usually in doubt—we go with the girl what brung us.

How we wind up choosing "liberal" or "conservative" as our default stance is part tribal. It also has to do with the life story we tell ourselves we are living out; when it comes to our character, "conservative" or "liberal" is part of the costume. Our default position can also reflect our relationship with a single, searingly important-to-us issue that's associated with one of the two general points of view.

It really doesn't matter how we come to identify with the "conservative" or "liberal" perspective. The trouble starts when we forget all of the stipulations above and start to think our political posture is truly connected with our inner life, or with moral philosophies that we imagine are more elaborate and essential to our soul than they really are. And everyone is so eager to defend their "core principles" that everybody forgets: our political stances are mostly just fallback positions.

This isn't an argument for moderate politics. Issue by issue, I believe that radical politics is often correct. I think hard-earned, deeply felt, and doggedly pursued personal political conviction is both effective and inspiring. Meanwhile, when someone proudly declares she's a "moderate," it sounds to me like someone who likes both the Cubs and the White Sox. Well, fine—I guess. But you're not really a baseball fan, and I don't want to talk to you about baseball.

Tiresome as it is, the liberal and conservative polarity endures because it is psychologically valid and intellectually useful. But if I'm gonna talk politics, I want to do it with people who force me to think harder than I normally do—and who remind me (over and over and over again) of the crucial difference between my real ideas and my assumed stances.

Do *You* "Vote Your Interests"?

W hen you stand in line to vote, how are you feeling? Eager to finally get your beak wet in the public trough? Or humbly virtuous because you're about to do the right thing, for the greater good?

One of the most stubborn and blind rhetorical canards of the white-collar Left about the working-class Right is: *They don't vote their interests.*

We Left pride ourselves on voting on principles and ideals and values. We boast about our magnanimous willingness to pay higher taxes for the common good. We accuse rich conservatives of selfishness—and then deride the working class on the Right for voting on a higher plane, in defense of ideals like freedom, family, and self-determination.

In her memoir *Heartland*, about growing up in Kansas, Sarah Smarsh points out that while liberals insist they be taxed to help the less fortunate, they leave "impoverished people"—working-class whites, in this case—to "do one of two things: Concede personal failure and vote for the party more inclined to assist them, or vote for the other party, whose rhetoric conveys hope that the labor of their lives is what will compensate them."

The Left must offer more to working-class whites and other disaffected Americans than promises of financial aid or government vocational training. It must appeal to their ideals and their pride and their deep wish to work for their bread—and it must appeal to their own generosity.

Because the chance to be noble drives poor people to the voting booth just like it drives the rest of us.

Liberal friends, we're very good at identifying rhetorical fallacies that come our way from the Right. We should make sure we're not firing dirty bombs back.

Hey, Washington:
This *Can* Go All the Way Bad

I once lived in a condo building that had seven units, on three levels. The two families on the ground level were sane. The three families on the top level were sane. The two people on the middle level were a little nutty to begin with, and they drove each other all the rest of the way insane.

By day, he was a thirtysomething, exacting, gossipy worrywart with an integrity problem. By night, he was a techno-music-partying maniac with a cocaine habit.

She, on the other hand, was a fearful, paranoid, middle-aged 24/7 grumbler who worried constantly, and correctly, that she had moved into the wrong building.

Our condo association meetings started out fun. Then they became dysfunctional. Then they ceased altogether.

Because whereas the rest of us briefly discussed and quickly voted on questions of building maintenance—whether or not we needed a new roof, whether we should hire someone to shovel the snow, how to resurface the hallway floor—the two middle-floor crazies worried those issues endlessly, discussing them at great length with one another in hallway whispers.

And then they fought over them, but not with one another—via email, or behind each other's backs in the kitchens of the sane people. This was entertaining, as each did manage to perfect a spot-on impression of the other. But ultimately it became exhausting and dispiriting.

After a couple of years, it became clear that we all had to move away, because these two had driven each other batshit, poisonous, total electrical meltdown, put-your-hand-on-the-hot-stove-because-you-think-it's-a-flower crazy. And their dynamic had permeated the entire building and all its inhabitants in such a way that we simply could not make sensible decisions, even though our own precious property value was at stake.

And so we all did. We all moved away.

That was a long time ago. I wonder why I keep thinking about it these days.

Republicans Have Feelings, Too

Despite my longtime loathing and sincere fear of President Trump, I have never turned in general on the people who voted for him. I still believe that one of the actions we can take as patriots is to communicate the very best we can, any chance we get, with people who are defining *patriotism* in a different way than we do. I'm talking not about convincing one another of our point of view—Lord knows, we've been trying that for long enough—but about forging some kind of mutually workable alternative to *this*.

But it's *hard*!

Very early in Trump's presidency, I managed to piss off one of the best-natured people I know, with a Facebook post about how I wish my male friends would stop "mansplaining to me how much calmer I ought to be" about the administration's activities.

Though I hadn't called him out or even hoped to draw him out, my friend correctly surmised that my post had been partly inspired by some posts he'd done doubting the wisdom and effectiveness of Trump's opposition.

No big deal, though, right? Good-natured guy, right? Point taken, right? Or, worst case, agree to disagree.

No. My friend got *mad*. How did I know he was mad? Because he said he wasn't mad. (I've been married a long time.)

Why was he mad? I think it was my use of the term *mansplaining* that really pissed him off.

Now, I thought it was kind of funny for a dude to complain about being mansplained to, and I actually thought it offered insight into one of the reasons I get so pissed off at conservatives. For all my life, conservative bosses, colleagues, family members, and friends have chuckled at me like they're my dad, explaining Fiscal Reality 101 to a third grader who wants a raise in his allowance to buy more candy. And I have resented it and often bitten my tongue. And I still resent it, as my oldest and dearest pal learned toward the end of a long night of drinking and condescension shortly after the 2016 election. I still remember the look of stunned surprise on his face when I erupted.

But I'd rather be called a naive fool than a heartless, ignorant prick. Which is what conservatives have been called *their* whole lives. Of course, they don't admit it hurts their feelings. Conservatives have felt resentment and bitten their tongues too. But *I don't care what people think* is the most frequently told human lie there is. And when they are accused of being sexist, racist, greedy, or selfish by someone they like—let alone called a "basket of deplorables" by someone they don't like—all those years of hurt come out. And usually they come out in the form of white-lipped rage.

Eventually, good-natured conservatives and good-natured liberals are going to have to talk to one another constructively, because we—not all of us, but some of us—are going to have to resolve national issues *together*. And we each need to be aware of not only the other person's old hurts, but our own.

Universities Are Not Safe Spaces

If you're making an effort to understand the depth of the political divide in America—and the hapless failure of even our best-educated and intellectually sophisticated citizens to communicate across it—you should spend some time with the doomed people who do public relations for universities.

I hold regular meetings for the people who help university presidents with their speeches and correspondence. Here are three facts university administrators deal with every day.

1. A lot of college students these days are nuts.

Some of them arrive on campus literally not understanding the basic tenets of free speech, and thus unprepared for the inevitable pain and discomfort of same. They behave as if they have never heard the quote wrongly attributed to Voltaire but rightly applied to the First Amendment: "I disapprove of what you say, but I will defend to the death your right to say it." So it's not necessarily liberal professors' fault that students are shouting down conservative speakers on campus. I don't remember when, in my childhood, I internalized *defend to the death your right to say it*, but college is a little too late to try to absorb an idea as fundamental as that.

2. Some (not most, but enough) professors are also nuts.

To hear Rush Limbaugh tell it, all they're doing at college these days is indoctrinating liberal snowflakes. Actually, they're doing all kinds of things, most of which have nothing to do with politics and everything to do with educating a class of people who can do the math, science, engineering, lawyering, reading, and leading to keep Americans' troubles first-world problems. But all you need is one tenured professor who is practicing "progressive stacking"—the nifty new trick of instructors correctively calling on minorities and women before whites and men—and Rush has a half-hour segment of glee, and his listeners have another legitimate reason to think the intellectuals have all gone mad.

3. University administrators have no idea what to do about any of it.

Remember "battle fatigue"? University administrators have "statement fatigue." These days, every university president has to deal on an exasperatingly regular basis with requests from student groups, faculty groups, parent groups, alumni, or community groups of two or two dozen or two hundred or two thousand, all of them demanding a *statement*—on any and all matters, ranging from a swastika drawn on a classroom wall to a national political crisis.

And do you know what happens in almost every one of these wearying cases? After days of the administrative frenzy necessary to craft and vet and recraft and re-vet such a statement, the group that demanded it complains bitterly that it doesn't go far enough. And the people who didn't think to demand a statement don't notice that it was ever issued, because they stopped reading these stupid statements—and everything else the university puts out—at least a year ago.

"What," yelled a participant at one of our meetings, over her own half-crazed cackle, "are we doing?"

At another meeting, our guest was Dr. Jonathan Zimmerman, professor of the history of education at the University of Pennsylvania and author of *Campus Politics: What Everyone Needs to Know.* I interviewed

Dr. Zimmerman about the modern campus life of trigger warnings, safe spaces, in loco parentis, microaggressions, sexual harassment, and hazing—a life I summed up by saying it's hard to tell the Ivy League from the bar in *Star Wars*.

Remember? "You will never find a more wretched hive of scum and villainy," Obi-Wan warns Luke as they walk into the bar. "We must be careful."

Dr. Zimmerman didn't disagree with my characterization.

No one did.

We must be careful.

What's Really "Deplorable"?
Taking Communication Out of Context

Gosh, I hate to rehash this.

Hillary Clinton may have gone about it clumsily—perhaps even oafishly—but she was actually trying to say she understood the perspective of many of the people who support a candidate whom she finds reprehensible.

Read the whole quote:

> You know, just to be grossly generalistic, you could put half of Trump's supporters into what I call the basket of deplorables. They're racist, sexist, homophobic, xenophobic, Islamophobic—you name it. And unfortunately there are people like that. And he has lifted them up. He has given voice to their websites that used to only have 11,000 people—now have 11 million. He tweets and retweets their offensive, hateful, mean-spirited rhetoric. Now some of these folks, they are irredeemable, but thankfully they are not America. But the other basket—and I know this because I see friends from all over America here—I see friends from Florida and Georgia and South Carolina and Texas as well as, you know, New York and California—but that other basket of people are people who feel that the government has let them down,

the economy has let them down, nobody cares about them, nobody worries about what happens to their lives and their futures, and they're just desperate for change. It doesn't really even matter where it comes from. They don't buy everything he says, but he seems to hold out some hope that their lives will be different. They won't wake up and see their jobs disappear, lose a kid to heroin, feel like they're in a dead end. Those are people we have to understand and empathize with as well.

Go find me a section of a Donald Trump speech where he tries to identify parts of Clinton's following, and asks his base to understand where they're coming from.

Now Clinton, for her part, could have tried a little harder. She could have at least acknowledged that some of Trump's following exists because she was the Studebaker that they've had for thirty years and they just wanted a different car.

Also, *irredeemable* is simply not an American term.

In her speech, was Clinton a little rough on the racists, sexists, homophobes, xenophobes, and Islamophobes that everybody knows are a part of Trump's following?

Did she overestimate their share among Trump's followers?

Should she have avoided putting groups of people in rhetorical "baskets"?

I don't know. I think I would have been tempted to go for the more alliterative "dumpster of deplorables."

In any case, the reason Clinton got hammered for her remark about the "basket of deplorables" is the very reason that *Vital Speeches of the Day* was founded. Back in 1934, Thomas Daly believed a large part of the nation's problems was the shortening, excerpting, and thus distorting of leaders' speeches in news reports. That's why Daly started his publication, declaring that "it is only in the unedited and unexpurgated speech that the view of the speaker is truly communicated to the reader."

This is why *Vital Speeches* still prints speeches in full and without commentary today. And in fact, this is why *Vital Speeches* still exists today. Not that we expect American citizens to hear a sound bite on Facebook and then go running to our website to read the speech stem to stern, the way they used to buy *Vital Speeches* off the newsstand. But future generations of scholars, when they research this bizarre political moment and every well-argued side of any issue, will be able—and thus will be obligated—to read the whole speech, and to see exactly what Hillary Clinton meant by "basket of deplorables" and what was the whole message she was trying to convey. These future scholars may conclude she was an arrogant elitist. Once they've read the whole speech, they'll have that right. But not until.

Here's what a speech is, friends, and what a speech will always be: A speech is when everybody sits down and shuts up for as long as the speaker talks. A speech is not just a series of stand-alone declarations (unless it's structured that way, in which case it's a crap speech). No, a speech is a whole argument, or a connected series of arguments, much more elaborate than a single phrase inside a single sentence. And when an audience member or media journalist is asked what a speech was about, that person should not say, "Aw, Clinton just called Trump supporters a basket of deplorables."

Because Clinton, in this case—and so many politicians in so many cases—did not "just" do any such thing. Any more than Mitt Romney, in 2012, "just" strutted out onto a debate stage and boasted that he had "binders full of women."

Alas, sound bite–snatching is human.

But reading the full text is divine.

We Know Bullshit Is Bad for Us,
but We Love the Taste

One thing public relations and marketing people know is, you *can* bullshit a bullshitter. That's because bullshitters allow themselves to be bullshitted just as easily as the next guy (who is usually something of a bullshitter himself).

Here's an example: Democratic politicians always talk about the middle class, rarely mention the working class, and almost never utter the word *poor*. That's because they don't want to remind everyone that there are poor people. In a hopeful-sounding campaign speech, it's a real buzzkill.

Yet reminding us there are poor people and proposing sensible ideas for dealing with poverty is ostensibly a main function of the Democratic Party. And wanting to alleviate poverty is one of the reasons many of us think we are Democrats, is it not?

I did not become a Democrat because I'm afraid that some middle-class factory worker will not be able to afford a new boat. I became a Democrat because I'm afraid she'll have her house foreclosed on and fall into poverty. And poverty sucks in this country—a lot less than it sucks in Haiti, but more than it sucks in anyone's dream of a great society.

And poverty is attached stubbornly to race, as anyone can see. "I think it's terribly sad that only Black people live in this neighborhood," my nine-year-old daughter said on a sortie down broken streets, past vacant lots, and between the rundown homes to the West Side Chicago school her mom teaches in. It's also terribly sad that Democratic politicians won't discuss the direct connection between race and poverty, which must be America's most stubborn shame.

It wasn't always this way. Franklin D. Roosevelt promised the Four Freedoms, one of which was freedom from want. Robert F. Kennedy talked about poverty, right down to the "dilapidated" housing in the "ghetto." Real stuff.

Democrats will bullshit us just as much as we let them. Let's stop letting them.

Well, what about Republicans? you say.

Let's politely set aside the outright lies that the Trump administration quickly got us accustomed to when it comes to the Republican Party. Let's envision a return to some semblance of normalcy in conservative rhetoric, and deal with that instead.

Even the most responsible Republicans pull a trick that we often fall for, for no good reason: they glorify small businesses. Why? So they don't have to glorify big businesses, which fund their campaigns, but which people resent for their impersonal power.

But in reality, if you're quantifying the qualities of businesses in general—well then, small businesses are as bad as big businesses, or worse.

You call the small firm "plucky"; I call it "underinsured."

You like the small company's hustle; I'm a little afraid of being hustled.

You like that you can deal with a human being; I often don't like the human being I'm dealing with, because I can hear in her voice the thinly veiled self-pity. She wishes she were somewhere else. She wishes she worked for, as she refers to it in happy-hour gripe sessions, a "real" company.

Small businesses—I'm talking twenty employees or fewer—are often lousy places to work: Boring, because unless the joint is on a massive growth binge, there's no place to go. Chaotic, if it is on a massive growth binge. Limited, because there isn't enough new blood to come up with new ideas, and there isn't enough capital to spend on them anyway.

Another problem with small businesses is that the boss has too much power. He or she constructs reality—a romantic history of the company, a fanciful description of the culture, a paranoid view of the marketplace, a sense of urgency wholly adjustable to his or her own anxiety level—and employees have to live in this world as if it is the actual world.

And unlike in larger organizations, where various departments and divisions work together on long-term plans arrived at by some consensus, there's nobody to tell the boss of a small business: *You've lost your mind.*

There are great small businesses to work in, and there are wise and thoughtful small-business owners to work for. In fact, I try to run one of those small businesses myself, with varying degrees of success. But my business, just because it is small, is not inherently better than a business that is big. Republicans know this, of course, but they say they're on the side of "small business" so they don't have to say, more straightforwardly, that they're pro-business in general.

Like Democrats, Republicans will bullshit us just as much as we let them.

Let's stop letting them.

Talking about Money
Is Talking about Feelings

My friend Adam Davidson writes about economics. He's good at it because he knows that economics is not about money. It's about people.

In a *New York Times Magazine* piece on immigration, he wrote about how we'd all be better off economically if we realized immigration is not a zero-sum game. It's not just a bunch of hungry foreigners taking a finite number of jobs from a finite number of American citizens. In a growing economy, immigration can *create* more jobs, by creating more demand for products and services and housing.

Most of us have heard this idea before, haven't we? So why don't we embrace it? Because even the way Adam backs it up with the work of economists, it seems a little reckless. It sounds like: *Let the hordes in! It'll probably be fine, and it might even be better!*

But no matter the theory, it always seems viscerally safer, even to the relatively comfortable readers of the *New York Times*, not to let the hordes in—even if the "hordes" aren't quite hordes. As Adam points out, even if the United States doubled the number of immigrant visas we issue, immigrants would still make up less than 0.7 percent of the workforce.

Why can't we get over our primal fears? We're people, not animals! Opening up our society to this modest group of productive people can fuel our economic growth. So why don't we smarten up?

Adam despairs:

> Whenever I'm tempted by the notion that humans are rational beings, carefully evaluating the world and acting in ways that maximize our happiness, I think of our meager immigration policies. For me, it's close to proof that we are, collectively, still jealous, nervous creatures, hoarding what we have, afraid of taking even the most promising risk, displaying loyalty to our own tribe while we stare, suspiciously, at everyone else.

It pains me a bit to say it, but I guess I don't share Adam's original ambition for the human race. I figure that people—just like animals on the Nature Channel—will *always* be nervous creatures, sleeping with one eye open, protective of their own asses and the asses of their loved ones over someone else's ass, and *certainly* over someone else's economic theory, however intellectually compelling.

When I was in my twenties and read about the famous first wave of "white flight" in the 1950s and 1960s—panicked people moving out of neighborhoods as minorities moved in, for fear that their property values would plummet—I held the cowardly homeowners partly to blame. Now that I am a homeowner (and a father), I understand how social virtue gets knocked out in the first round by the gnawing fear of your own obsolescence and your fond dreams for your children. Had my property value been threatened—or had I believed it was—I have very little confidence that I would have behaved any differently, and I'm not ashamed to say so despite all my fancy enlightened attitudes about fairness and race and cultural diversity.

Someone who wants to change immigration policy, or any other economic policy, mustn't dismiss people's fear and greed. Nor is it wise to dismiss their other feelings of virtuous, welcoming generosity. Because far from being a rational subject, economics brings out the very most irrational, fight-or-flight, self-preserving parts of people—and their self-righteousness, too.

Economics is food and shelter and safety from harm. All the economic education and communication in the world won't make people think intellectually about that.

Why I Like Politicians

In a representative democracy, how do patriots reconcile the fact that they hate politicians—both those they have elected and those they will elect in the future? They don't reconcile it. But they just go on hating politicians anyway.

I happen to like politicians. Sometimes I like them more as campaigners than as office holders. Other times I actually like them better in office.

But the truth is, I like politicians in general. As people. So when, say, a woman sits down next to me at a dinner party and I ask her what she does, and she says she's an elected official, I say, "Great!"

As a writer, I've interviewed many politicians. Also, I had a close friend who became an elected official, and I watched him work—in parades, at fundraisers, at Greek diners in small towns. I saw him pumping hands, asking questions, taking notes, remembering names.

Here's what I like about politicians.

They are willing to meet with people.
Politicians encounter dozens of people every day, hundreds every month, and thousands every year—and hear about their troubles, from all their stupefyingly various and often downright kooky points of view. Go ahead and chalk up their motive to getting reelected, but not before you ask yourself how many interviews *you'd* be willing to have to get a job.

They think about what you think.

Politicians think less about their own opinions than about yours. This is what it means to be "political"—and it means the more political a person is, the better the politician.

They ask for what they want.

A politician is used to looking you right in the eye and asking for your support, your money, your vote. As Steve Goodman sang, "That's not an easy thing to do." When was the last time you did it?

They try to figure out which words people like best.

Politicians stand up and make speeches to please your ears and the mind in between them. As a writer, how can I not appreciate that? As a parent, teacher, coach, or boss—how can you not appreciate it?

They work very, very hard.

I once interviewed a dozen ex-politicians for a story about life after politics. Just about every one said that life after politics is a breeze, and one of these guys is a corporate CEO.

They don't spend a lot of time thinking about what the perfect job for them would be.

Politicians live a wild and unpredictable existence—at the mercy of mad electoral mood swings, at the center of constantly shifting power dynamics, always either in the spotlight or in range of a searchlight. If this makes them less introspective or suits a less bookish type of person . . . well, what of it?

They aren't as solely self-interested as you think.

I heard a cable news commentator ask rhetorically how senators and congressmen can be so "spineless." The commentator was simply asking the question we all wonder about sometimes: *Are those jobs just so great that holding on to them is worth losing one's integrity and reputation?*

I used to shake my head similarly, until I got acquainted with a few politicians and realized that a politician's job isn't just a job. For better or for worse, these are small kingdoms. They are communities, they are movements, and they are a big part of people's lives—not just the politician's life.

Asking any nationally elected politician to resign or cast a suicidal vote means asking her, first of all, to lay off many staffers . . . and to let down the supporters who knocked on their neighbors' doors and vouched for their friend . . . and to let the air out of a balloon they and hundreds or thousands of people have filled with their life's breath for years or even decades.

When a politician contemplates career suicide, she surely thinks as much about the people she'll leave behind—who also happen to be all the friends she has in the world. And so maybe it's not surprising to see that she doesn't think about career suicide much at all.

———

I don't wish everybody was a politician. I'm just glad some people are, because somebody needs to be.

Sympathizing with politicians doesn't mean indulging bums with my vote. But understanding them as the fallible fellow citizens they are—rather than aliens dropped down to rule us from the Planet Moron—gets us a little closer to the way we're supposed to see them, and treat them, in the first place.

And Seriously:
Stop Calling the People Names

My old man passed on some advice that probably sounded old-fashioned when his own father gave it to him, in the 1930s: "Preface everything you say with 'I think.'"

Or as my writer friend Mike Long says in his plummy southeastern Missouri drawl, "Nobody ever won an argument by starting with 'Hey, Stupid.'"

Yet all the time, I see my liberal friends (and occasionally my conservative friends) write phrases on Facebook like *Trump supporters are fucking idiots*. Call me a snowflake, but even as a Trump-loathing libtard, that upsets me.

Let's break that down.

Why do I think it's OK to call myself "Trump-loathing"? Because I do loathe Trump. I didn't like the cut of his jib when he owned the New Jersey Generals in the United States Football League. I thought every building he put up was tacky and everything he said was vulgar. I was glad when he went bankrupt in the 1990s, and by the time he started running for president, I had considered him a tasteless blight on American culture for at least a quarter of a century. In fact, I loathe him so thoroughly that sure, yes—I do sometimes struggle to imagine how a large number of my fellow American citizens think he's just the greatest. It feels like accepting that some people just like to eat charcoal: they like the taste, they like the texture, and they think it cleans out their system. Go figure!

But since we *are* talking about a high percentage of my fellow citizens, I must accept the possibility—indeed, the probability—that part of the problem here is a failure of my own imagination.

In fact, I fervently *hope* this is the problem, because the alternative—that more than a third of our country are intellectually and morally insensate savages—would be more than painful to accept. It would be impossible to deal with and still call myself an American patriot.

Despite my struggle to understand them, I personally know some Trump supporters whom I truly like. And even if I didn't, I couldn't call them names until I'd met them all and walked a mile in their skins—as every liberal's moral dad, Atticus Finch, advises.

And so I don't call Trump supporters names.

And so I take my Chicago-raised, politically cloistered teenage daughter on backroads through the countryside so she can see that Trump supporters might serve you pancakes and offer you whipped cream for your hot chocolate and smile and call you *hon*.

And so I embrace insights like the one uttered by the former political operative Dan Gerstein at a speechwriting conference: During the 2016 campaign, "Hillary Clinton told a thousand truths in the service of one lie"—that things in America were essentially hunky-dory. Meanwhile, "Trump told a thousand lies in the service of what sounded to many ears like one truth"—that once-plentiful manufacturing, farming, and coal-mining jobs had been replaced by nothing but misery and opioids and neglect by Washington.

"I have been talking about helping coal country for a very long time," Hillary Clinton said wearily in 2016. Trump at least had the courtesy to promise coal miners they'd get their jobs back. And if you think they were idiots to believe him—well, haven't you ever voted for a politician just for putting your fondest hope into words? Just for *saying it*? I have.

In any case, at a politically explosive moment in American history, calling millions of strangers "idiots" on social media sounds to me like yelling *Fire!* in a crowded theater—or at least shouting *Redneck!* in a rural one.

As the writer David Wong said, "It feels good to dismiss people, to mock them, to write them off as deplorables. But you might as well take time to try to understand them, because I'm telling you, they'll still be around long after Trump is gone."

And they'll remember what you said.

My old man used to quote some musician: "You can say what you want with a slide trombone, but with words you've got to be careful."

A speaker at the first World Conference of the Professional Speechwriters Association sounded an even more cautionary tone. "When a word goes into the universe, it doesn't go away," said Jeff Ansell, a communication coach. "It reverberates around the universe forever."

I can't prove words stay in the universe forever. But I can't figure out how they would get out.

When my daughter was in fourth grade, she received a related lesson from her teacher, about bullying. Mr. Johnson told the class that as a child, he had been bullied and called names. He held up a piece of paper, crumpled it up, and then uncrumpled it. He said the names he had been called are like the lines in the uncrumpled paper: "They never go away."

"Dad, isn't that brilliant?" my daughter said that evening. She was nine.

I think we all have some growing up to do, and I hope it's not too late.

V.

MONDAY, TUESDAY, WEDNESDAY, THURSDAY, FRIDAY: COMMUNICATING WITH YOUR COLLEAGUES

My parents took their work seriously.

My mother was a novelist, and when we were little, she paid a babysitter to watch us in the mornings while she was writing, so she could hear herself think over the hum of her IBM Selectric. Her office door was *closed*, like a bank vault is closed, and before we knocked on it, both we and the babysitter knew we'd better be sure our problem was more important than what was going on in there. And a skinned knee did not qualify.

My father was in advertising, and I wrote a book about his career, whose prime ran parallel with Don Draper's in the TV series *Mad Men*. Except, as I discovered while researching my book, my dad and his colleagues at General Motors' Detroit ad agency Campbell Ewald didn't dissipate themselves with sex and booze. They blew off steam through *memos*.

Campbell Ewald's president, the creative director, and the copy supervisors typed—and their secretaries retyped—frequent, long, searching, urgent, and occasionally heated intra-office exchanges about advertising theory and the implications of the creative revolution that was spreading from New York to other agencies around the country.

And no one wrote more of these memos than Tom Murray, even as a midlevel copy supervisor.

"I think our present GM advertising, while adequate, is neither portraying the kind of image GM should be portraying nor does it agree with the kind of image the products themselves represent," my dad wrote to his boss, creative director Kensinger Jones, in 1960. "In short, I think our ads look like the nineteen thirties or early forties in the magazines, yet we are offering for sale the newest cars made in the world today. The ads, in other words, look like the GM Building when they should look like the cars."

In memo after hectoring memo, this ambitious young executive with a family to feed and a mortgage to pay challenged (and probably annoyed) his bosses to find ways to recruit more creative people. He proposed ways to find less stodgy clients. He agitated for *progress*, as he saw it—progress, for its own sake.

Why?

Because he saw his work as a huge part of his whole contribution as a person, and he knew if he was going to leave his mark in the world, his office was one of the likeliest locations.

I'm giving over a section of this book to "communicating with your colleagues" not because I want to take the American work culture back to the days of Don Draper—or even to the mores of macho workahol-ics like Jack Welch or Steve Jobs. It's because I think that work, and the work relationships we form in reasonably healthy organizations, is one of the most reliable ways to be happy—with our country, with our fellow human beings, with ourselves. Or to be less unhappy, anyway.

Work is where we show up for one another every single day, where we can not only express but also demonstrate—in the most concrete ways— concern for one another. And candor. And good humor. And kindness. Not only do these qualities make good colleagues; they make good friends. They make people happy. And given the right circumstances, they're easier to achieve at work than anywhere else. Because work is the real life where we can prove our loyalty, earn lasting trust, and offer our generosity and our good nature to one another. Work is where we can receive the benefits of our colleagues' beauty in real and truly useful ways.

Of course, it doesn't always work out that way—and when it doesn't, our job can also be draining and exhausting and enraging and devastating.

It can make your whole life seem meaningless and can even poison the way you think about our whole society and our whole country. So it seems like we ought to talk about ways to communicate with our colleagues better—more trustingly, more deeply, more courteously, and more courageously.

Working on Eggshells

It's said that in an unhappy marriage, loud arguments frequently erupt or cold silences commence because in an unhappy marriage, everything is about everything.

"Pass the salt" means *You're a terrible cook!*

"I'd rather not go until Christmas Eve" means *You hate my family!*

"Let's wait until next month to buy the duvet cover" means *You don't trust me with money!*

All of society is starting to feel like that. Now we are reading serious articles advising us on safe topics of conversation at family dinners, and we focus our precious human imaginations on the art of being amusing, yet sufficiently banal that no one could object.

The most reliable way I can witness and understand the profundity of this change is from my own little world: the society of a couple hundred thousand Americans who make a living in the business of corporate communication. I once wrote trade publications for these people, and for the first ten or fifteen years of my career—roughly the early 1990s to the mid-2000s—professional arguments were robust, common, and usually fun. These natural and necessary exchanges took place first in the opinion columns and letters sections of industry newsletters and at industry conferences, then on rudimentary internet forums with ungainly names like PRSIG, and eventually in the comments sections of blogs written by people prominent in the profession.

We discussed such questions as:

Whom does an employee want to hear from first: his or her direct super-visor, or the CEO?

Should employee publications continue to publish personal stories about employees, or should these publications be strictly business?

Is the news release dead? Is print dead? Is face-to-face communication dead? Is public relations dead?

Is it possible to quantify the bottom-line impact of communication?

Is a particular communication ethics principle worth quitting your job over?

These and dozens of other topics regularly generated sometimes noisy debates and occasionally deafening donnybrooks characterized by accusations of *You just set corporate communication back thirty years.* There were bruised feelings. There were participants so stubborn and tunnel-visioned that they might now be called "trolls." And there was seldom resolution.

But there *was* something that amounted to an ongoing and evolving philosophical debate on the nature and purpose of corporate communication.

For several years now—unless in my own tunnel vision, I fail to know its location—there is almost *no* such debate. Why?

A few reasons. First of all, when those debates were taking place, people generally had more job security. They were a little less fearful of burning a bridge and thus more willing to risk rubbing a colleague the wrong way or expressing an unpopular opinion.

Plus, because they often had a stronger connection to a longtime employer, people tended to *care more*—about their institutions and about the profession they worked in. They were more inclined to spend the time and spill the blood. People who run professional associations complain that it's harder these days to get folks to volunteer for board positions. The official explanation is that everyone's too busy, but that really means they don't give a shit.

But one other reason may be more important than both of those: back then, arguing about communication wasn't arguing about *everything*. For instance, I could (and frequently did) have an argument with the profession's leading tech guru about our widely differing beliefs in technology as a solution to age-old communication ills. It never occurred to either of us to broaden the argument to something like *Well, of course you would think that, because of [your politics, your vanity, your function as an unthinking tool of the great oligarchy]*. No. An argument about communication was an argument about communication, and it had to be won or lost or drawn on its own merits.

Doesn't it sound now like I'm describing the peculiar cultural manners of the Edwardians a full century ago? But it was only fifteen years ago that these debates and the diversity of debaters began to dwindle. This sort of discussion was engaged by fewer working practitioners and left mostly to pundits like me and a handful of consultants whose public engagement was a natural part of their self-promotion.

When did the professional debate begin to blink out entirely? Maybe it was about the time that the 2008 recession scared the professional bejeezus out of everyone and left us huddled together on LinkedIn right in the middle of a US presidential election that polarized the country in new ways.

In any case, I can't remember the last time I had a lively public exchange of ideas about communication. I bet you've experienced something similar in your line of work. Because whatever your industry, you're mincing along with everybody else up to a single water cooler: LinkedIn.

LinkedIn is where everyone is delighted to be invited into the winter aspen forest of exclamation points and lavish "likes" and logrolling: *I'll endorse your core competencies if you'll endorse mine*. It's where we share counterfeit kudos: *Congrats on twenty-two years at the Department of Streets and Sanitation!* It's where we release "exciting news," like a notification that the dog kennel you work at has been around for fifteen years. Claptrap is king: *It's never about the role and always about the goal*. And the most courageous stances you'll see are in favor of such controversial positions as lifelong learning, leadership, excellence, and work-life balance.

No wonder Americans so frequently accuse each other of being full of shit. We are!

If we can't muster the caring or the courage to start serious conversations on the meaning and purpose of the work we do, can we at least stop blowing so much smoke up each other's asses?

Real Bonding in a Virtual World

Years ago, when my buddy Tony Judge lived here in Chicago's Ukrainian Village, he would call me up after dinner on a winter's weeknight and say, "I sure could use to see Hertha." Hertha Rojek was the bartender at the J&M Tap, a corner tavern that stood almost exactly the same number of paces between my house and Tony's. I would hem for a second, haw for another, then put down my book and pull on my boots.

Tony and I talked about a lot of things over those quiet weeknight beers, but one of the things we talked about most was communication—specifically, email and other electronic communication, and how it was destroying the world, at least as far as Tony was concerned.

For forty years, Tony had earned his living as an arts fundraiser and public radio underwriting salesman, among many other things—he was also Studs Terkel's cornerman and Garrison Keillor's front man. Tony succeeded in his work by making relationships—friendly, funny, smart, inside-jokey, often whiskey-lubricated friendships—with dozens and dozens and dozens of the right people in Chicago and around the world. At the height of his long career, Tony had as many real-life friends as you have Facebook friends. He used that personal network to connect creative people with money people and get paid in the process.

It's hard to be a professional schmoozer over email.

Tony felt that more than making his personal form of relationship-building obsolete, people's reliance on electronic communication and their increasing reluctance to meet face-to-face and talk on the phone have hurt the economy. From his perspective, this technology is making business relationships shallow and emotionally flat—more impermanent, less productive, less rich, and ultimately less rewarding.

I thought Tony's theory was a little self-serving, and I think his old-fashioned bonding method can be chummy to the point of corrosive; this is how old boys' networks get built. But I was (and still am) also troubled by the gathering group of people who don't seem to know when personal contact is called for. I wrote this snotty little thing back in 2014:

> The Cambridge Dictionary calls the use of "mute" as a noun "old-fashioned, offensive." But I'm bringing the term up to date, by applying it to some modern young people, who are tragically unable to use the telephone or call a face-to-face meeting for any purpose. They are the New Mutes.
>
> Before sign language was invented, people who couldn't speak had to scribble what they wanted to say on pads of paper. It must have been a halting way to carry on a conversation.
>
> The New Mutes have better tools than pads of paper. They have email, instant messaging, Tweeting, and texting, all of which make it easier to communicate more rapidly than the furious scribbling and pad-passing of the past.
>
> But alas, the New Mute is still mute—unable to convey meaning or feeling by tone of voice or body language or facial expression. It is not known whether the New Mutes are unaware of the crucial uses of these basic human tools or merely unable to employ them. Whatever the case, the result is the same: The New Mutes are entirely dependent on what they say and unable to control how they say it, beyond the blunt and banal use of exclamation points and emoticons! :(
>
> Thus, they cannot effectively inspire, soothe, convince, scare, or motivate colleagues or customers. They can only nag their correspondents, irritate them, and make them nervous

with flat lines like *Hope that helps!* and *Thanks so much!* and *You rock!* A New Mute I was corresponding with recently had "Thanks for your patience!" *as part of her auto signature.*

Despite such profound limitations, the New Mutes work courageously right alongside their talking colleagues in corporations, government organizations, universities, and charities. Some types of work they do just as effectively as their talking colleagues.

Alas, another kind of work—the little matter of building rich, trusting relationships that lead to innovation and lasting bonds that connect organizations, industries, and nations to build the world economy and hold human society together—is obviously far beyond the capabilities of the New Mutes.

Perhaps the New Mutes should be covered by the Americans with Disabilities Act, and not be pitied for what they cannot do, but rather honored for the courage they show when occasionally invited to a mandatory meeting or pressured into physically attending a colleague's birthday lunch. Or maybe they should just learn sign language.

Or maybe they should be taught, for their own good—by elder colleagues who would probably prefer to scratch their heads in self-righteous bewilderment—that some kinds of communication must, absolutely, positively, no doubt about it, be done in person.

The School for the Rehabilitation of the New Mutes, for instance, will not offer a correspondence course.

Since I wrote that, Tony moved to Massachusetts, and I have worked full time with someone who lives 1,750 miles away in Phoenix, Arizona. Most of our communications are electronic, and it is the single most meaningful professional relationship I have ever had.

Benjamine Knight is the chief operating officer of the company I run. She oversees all the administration of *Vital Speeches of the Day* magazine; the Professional Speechwriters Association; all the events we put on; and our events program, the Cicero Speechwriting Awards. You wouldn't actually believe how much she does for this little company.

When Benjamine and I began working together, I assumed the physical distance between us would necessarily limit the nature of our partnership to functional, collegial professionalism. That beats the hell out of its opposite. But it does not build an organization the way that Benjamine and I—to both of our delight—have gone on to build ours.

Isn't it a bit sterile and quiet and emotionally flat to instant message our way through every day? It would be, if we didn't do a few other simple things.

We talk every week on the phone—during a two-hour, two-person "staff meeting," where we always spend the first fifteen or twenty minutes catching each other up on our personal lives. We spend longer if a family member has cancer or if we just got back from vacation, but almost never shorter—no matter how busy we are. We want to do this, and I think we instinctively knew we had to do this, to become real to one another, and to remind each other of our homely humanity.

I have a weird rash on my arm that I'll get checked out if it doesn't clear up by tomorrow.

Her new couch is coming today—finally!

I'm not a big fan of my teenage daughter's boyfriend.

She's worried about her mother's health.

We see each other six times a year in person, at our own conferences and seminars, and also at an annual planning session in Chicago or Phoenix. Mixing with one another—and meeting our customers and partners together in person—deepens our bond as we develop shared colleagues, traditions, jokes, references, and institutional lore, which are the building blocks of culture.

There was the time in Montreal when our conference was about to start but the two of us were locked in a stairwell.

And the seminar in Chicago where I thought to clear the food off the table to make room for the afternoon snack—and then realized that what I'd scraped into the trash can *was* the afternoon snack.

And the time I publicly thanked her at the end of the World Conference of the Professional Speechwriters Association for being such a mensch, and I cried in front of the whole assembly. Oh right, that's every time. And you can't do it on IM.

What you *can* do on IM is be accountable to one another day to day and hour to hour. When Benjamine starts work in the morning—a couple of hours after I start, thanks to the time difference—she says good morning before any business communication begins. If I'm going to go for a midday run, I tell her I'm taking a break and ask if there's anything she needs from me first. And always—*always*—we check in before we close down for the day, asking one another if there's anything more we need, and sharing our plans for the evening, even if they only amount to reading a book or watching TV.

Day by day, over many weeks and several years, we have become such experts in the rhythms of one another's lives and tones of voice (even on IM) that it's hard for either of us to conceal anything from one another—a hangover, a day of feeling overwhelmed, or an occasional afternoon when we just don't give a shit. So we rarely even bother to try.

Benjamine and I are very different people. In some important ways, we are opposites, and not natural soul mates by any means. But we complement each other uncannily, and we know a couple things in common: how to work like hell and what it takes to keep in real touch with another person.

Such work relationships may be uncommon, but if they occur less than they used to, it's not technology getting in between people who want to connect. It's *reticent people* who don't want to connect, who use technology and distance and emotional detachment to maintain that it's just business, just a job, and just a paycheck—and to hide their eyes. Because they are afraid, for the reasons all people have ever been afraid, of giving deep parts of themselves to their work or their colleagues. Connection is a good way to get hurt, get taken advantage of, or have your time wasted right before HR calls you into a meeting and tells you to pack up your shit and leave.

Alas, working with your heart in it is also the only way to make your workweek a meaningful part of your life. It's the only way to do work that amounts to anything in the end.

So Benjamine and I, we take that chance.

As for Tony, he and I miss Hertha, who left the J&M Tap and took a job working for the TSA at O'Hare Airport. "I like people," she explained, hopefully.

Tony and I remember our nights at the J&M fondly. They helped us build a bond personal enough to survive most of the year on phone calls and text messages. I visit Tony sometimes, and when he comes to Chicago, he stays with me, and we walk down to the J&M together.

Tech, as in Wreck

We really need to use communication technology more wisely and sensitively. Failing to do so adds significantly to the trouble we have with one another, not only in the workplace—thousands of couples are fighting like rabid wolverines over text as I write this—but *often* in the workplace. Think about the rapacious reply alls. The backbiting bccs. Those 2:00 a.m. emails from bosses who "don't expect a reply right now" (and from those fuckheads who do).

We have enough substantive quarrels in this world. If we can alleviate conflict and promote communication at work (and at home) simply by using a different medium or saying things in a different way, we should.

Voice Mail Should Go the Way of the Fax.
Voice mail fills me with crawling dread, because as we all know, it is by voice mail that catastrophic news will come.

Enter your password, followed by the pound sign.

A dozen rifles cock.

If you want to listen to your messages, press one.

What do I press if I want to jump out the window?

You have seven voice mail messages.

Oh shit, that's exactly the number of clients I have—or had. The photo of me in assless chaps must have hit the papers.

The best-case scenario is when you brace yourself for disaster, only to find out that six of the messages are automated recordings from Chicago

Public Schools telling you to bundle up your kid because it's cold outside. The seventh is from a client or colleague who merely identifies himself or herself and says, "Give me a call when you can."

With so many other means of more detailed and ball-advancing query-making now, a voice mail message to "call me" seems like a manipulative stunt that you wouldn't think of pulling on email or text, unless you were somebody's inconsiderate boss or impatient spouse. But somehow it's still acceptable on voice mail—the way a ransom note is still acceptable over fax, I guess.

Why wouldn't you tell me why you're calling? Is it because you think *just wanna catch up* isn't urgent-sounding enough to get you the callback? Meanwhile, you're leaving me to think maybe poor Uncle Frank finally died—only to find out that you just have the dialies because you're stuck in traffic somewhere.

Or are you giving me only a *Give me a call* message because you want to spring something on me in person? Or because you don't want to give me time to prepare an excuse for why I can't come to your family's Easter dinner? Or perhaps you know perfectly well why, but you still want to hear me say, "Because I'm watching the Masters instead." Or you want to catch me off guard in some other way.

No. I won't give you a call. Because I think you're going to surprise me with something, and I don't like surprises. I'm a complicated guy, living a busy life in a complicated world! I don't just answer all questions and take all comers and return all phone calls just because the caller told me to!

I'm thinking about changing my outgoing message:

> Hi, this is David Murray. I can't talk right now, and I don't check voice mail because voice mail is used these days only to deliver messages of doom, or to manipulate people. I hope you'll email or text me the reason for your call, and if it seems as urgent to me as it does to you, I'll call you back as soon as I can.

You may think voice mail isn't worthy of such fear and loathing. Email me all about it.

Email Auto-Reply Is a Political Act.

"I am out of the office and not checking email," the magazine editor's auto-reply said abruptly. "I will return Tuesday, March 24. Anything sent during this time will not be read."

Having spent a hunk of a week digging out from an email blizzard that had accumulated while I was gone for two weeks, I stand and applaud this editor's declaration of independence from emails sent while he's on vacation. *If you want to reach me so damn bad,* he is saying, *you'll write me again when I'm back.*

And I do. And I will! In fact, I'll wait until a little later in the week, when I figure he'll have regained his stride.

Every job has its own proper sense of urgency, and the requirement for responsiveness varies. Editors can afford to acknowledge correspondents on their own time; plumbing contractors cannot (and IT people cannot, but they do anyway).

But when it comes to evenings, weekends, or weeks away, each of us must cultivate our own sense of confidence—that we're worth waiting a week for, that the work will be there when we return, that we deserve time away because we are not twenty-four-hour-a-day, seven-day-a-week air traffic controllers or 911 operators.

In my younger writing days, when *freelance* was just another word for nothing left to lose, I used to say on my auto-reply that I'd be hard to reach because I was "on a ramble." I always thought clients would think that was cool.

Now that I own one good suit and run an organization with *Professional* in the title, I usually say on my auto-reply that I'll be checking email occasionally, but unless the matter is urgent—and really, how urgent can writing about rhetoric be?—let's connect next week.

That line almost puts the onus back on my correspondent to check back in with me next week. And it certainly gives me the breathing room I need to be away when I'm away as thoroughly as I'm here when I'm here—which is exactly what I'm after.

Am I overthinking this? As a child, a friend once accused his brother of overthinking something.

"I'm not overthinkin' it," his brother cried. "I'm just thinkin' it!"

When People Don't Respond to Your Emails—It's Not You, It's Them.
I'm a professional idea person, provocateur, salesman, and convener.

I send several dozen emails most days, as it usually turns out. It was forty-five yesterday, and that wasn't a heavy day. (I say "turns out" because if I actually knew every morning that I had fifty or sixty emails to send that day, I would stay under the covers. In fact, I'm now thinking of going back to bed.)

Lots of times I send emails that don't require a response, and yet I wind up receiving a long response. Occasionally I'll query someone I don't expect to hear back from right away, but I do hear from that person. And sometimes I write to people who don't think I'm important enough to compel a reply, and it turns out that I'm right.

Occasionally, though, I send emails that I'm pretty sure will get a response, and they don't.

Why?

Is it because I wrote something unforgivably thoughtless and barbaric that I, through the one-way mirror of my own narcissism, could not see?

Or is it because the person has only barely tolerated me heretofore, and when she replied to my previous email, she swore it would be the last?

Really, those are the only two choices.

Except that, 999 times out of 1,000, the truth is something else: My email is stuck in the other person's spam folder. The other person has been on a massive deadline or an alcoholic bender. The other person needs to check with his boss. The other person was waiting for a suitable time to write me a thoughtful reply. Or the other person has been shopping my email to Hollywood because he thinks it would make a great feature film.

Once, very early in my journalism career, I sent a hard-wrought, heavy-duty 6,000-word cover story to the magazine editor who had commissioned it. I didn't hear back for two weeks despite sending several follow-up emails. Finally, unable to take it anymore, I e-blurted, "I know the piece isn't right! It's not structured right, it's not conceived right, it has no heart, and it puts forth no central idea and draws no conclusion! I need to rewrite it, and I need your help. Please let me know when we can meet."

"Sorry, I was on vacation," he said. "The piece is great. When can you sit for your author's headshot?"

Rhetoric and Bullshit: The Difference

I'm a communicator, not a crook.

That doesn't mean I'm any kind of a paragon of straight talk. A search of any day's emails or a transcript of a week's phone calls would show me buttering up and building up, getting a leg up and rushing past objections. You'd see me expressing more interest than I have, asking for more rope than I deserve, giving myself the benefit of the doubt, trying to close the deal.

I'm a salesman just like the next guy: I'm selling my writing, I'm selling my conferences, I'm selling myself—all day long, just like you. I'm selling this idea, right now—to both of us.

But I'm doing it *as straight as I possibly can*, and usually *with the expectation that I'm going to know you for the rest of my life* so I have to be careful not to say anything truly bullshitty *that I'll forget to say the next time we talk, or another time we talk, ten years from now.*

The other day I was writing to a business associate about a situation in which his feelings may have been bruised. I was at pains to make him understand how much I appreciated a generous offer he had made me that I had reluctantly turned down for a better one. I wrote, *You're the best friend I have in this business.* Then I looked at the sentence and asked: Was it true? I made an inventory of my other good friends in that sphere of my life. Were any of them better friends than this guy? No, they were not. And of course, a tie goes to the writer. So I left the sentence in the email and felt good about sending it.

I'm not a communication saint, but I'm not a real sinner, either.

In business situations where I've been surrounded by crooks or expected to be one—usually when buying something I don't know the value of, or selling something whose value I doubt—I have been a terrible, terrible failure. I've constantly revealed things I shouldn't have revealed. Whenever it's been my turn to talk, I've generally failed to be sufficiently convincing.

Eventually, stubbornly, and not as a result of moral righteousness but as a result of embarrassing failure, I have been forced to conclude that I am perfectly, even exceptionally, good at articulating, amplifying, or even exaggerating a version of a thing that I consider the truth. And—possibly because I am lazy or stupid—I am worse than anyone at constructing or camouflaging or minimizing a thing I think is false.

So I need to make my home in a relatively honest industry. I need to surround myself with shooters who are at least as straight as me—people who are actually out to get what they say they're out to get, and people who want from me that which I am prepared to give, in exchange for a price they're willing to pay.

Which limits my options, let me tell you—in business and in the rest of my life.

But there it is: the truth.

Kids Learn about Sex from Each Other—but How Do They Learn about Work?

If I could magically give my daughter one gift in life, it would be that she finds a meaningful kind of work that can lead her through a coherent (however winding) career. Having such work carries you through thick times and thin. It guides you, distracts you, engages your body and soul on Monday, Tuesday, Wednesday, Thursday, and Friday. And thus it gives substance to your weekends, too.

If you're not afraid of work, you'll be OK in life—and if you *like* to work, you will be happy. And if you don't? Well, you're in trouble and I feel sorry for you, even if you've got a billion dollars. I mean, what are you going to do all day, water-ski?

I've had ups and downs in my career, but I've always had useful work to do. It's what I'm most grateful for, to God. Wait, was it God that gave me this gift of good work, or was it my parents? After all, both were writers—and especially my dad, who talked all the time about his career and his daily work at the ad agency.

Long before I was ten years old, I knew every client of my dad's ad agency, which writers were assigned to each client, and who was succeeding (and who was not). I knew who was boring my dad in meetings, who was taking credit for his work, who was spending too much on the expense account, and who was carrying the agency on his back. I knew enough to exult when the agency lost the Brown Derby restaurant account because the client was a crazy asshole. Well, I may have not known *all* of those things, but I knew most of them.

Knowing that stuff at age eight, nine, ten strikes me as a little weird now—didn't Dad have anybody else to talk to?—but I bet I learned an awful lot from all that premature work talk. Most of all, I learned that work was an important part of a good life.

Yet it has not been my instinct to have my daughter read a lot of my writing, or even to explain to her why I'm happy to have something I wrote in the *New York Times*. By now she has seen my name in a lot of magazines and newspapers, and my picture in a few too. She thinks I'm famous, but she has absolutely no sense of how famous on a scale from Bruno Mars to Uncle Mike (of Uncle Mike's Café, around the corner).

She knows that I write and that I deal with speechwriters, but that's about it. I'm not moved to tell her yarns about all the interesting speech-writers I know (though she's been out to dinner with a few of them). And she doesn't seem to give a natural shit about it either. When she was twelve, I set before her a magazine article with my mug on it and the headline "The speechwriters' shepherd: David Murray gathers wandering professionals into a coherent community."

She saw my picture and said, "Cool." Then she put the magazine aside.

She knows that I have a blog and some people read it, and that I sometimes post about her and they think she's amusing. And if I'm writ-ing about something less esoteric than communication, I'll tell her about that, too.

Once, we were together when I received an email from a university student, asking for career advice. "Dad, that's amazing!" she said with genuine surprise and admiration. "People go to you for advice!"

But mostly she tells me she feels sorry for me, because she sees me at my desk when she leaves for school in the morning, and again when she returns home after soccer practice. "You do the same thing *every single day*."

Which is a tragic fate to befall the man she knows is the greatest historian, oral reader, tennis player, golfer, bicyclist, motorcyclist, milkshake drinker, and comedian she has ever known, not to mention farter.

But as for the larger task of sharing the meaning of my work with her, and telling her what it means to me, I don't *exactly* know how to go about it. Because—like my longstanding plan to take her to hear the best rabbis, priests, and Baptist preachers around town—I think I ought to do it, I've always intended to do it, but it doesn't come naturally.

And time is running out.

Now she's seventeen, and the adolescent attention vortex has descended.

When I told her I'd found a publisher for this book, she hesitated, and then asked apologetically, "What book?"

Working with the Enemy

I talked already about Benjamine. My company's other main contributor—our accountant and magazine fulfillment director—is a suburban Republican guy who voted for Trump at least once and probably twice.

Why don't I know for sure? Because I could not care less.

Why not? Because Mike is the most relentlessly cheerful guy I know.

He is capable. Reliable. Honest. Wise. Loyal in ways that I am not, in ways that make me sit and wonder—in ways that threaten his own livelihood. And he's funny. Like, college-buddy funny. Ask him sometime what it means to be "shit-grabbing mad."

He's available for any problem or question or asinine brainstorm or expression of anxiety, anytime. Vulnerable—in a good way—and willing to share his own miseries. A mensch and a friend whom I've known for twenty-five years and to whom I get closer the more time we spend together—with still a long way to go, I hope.

As for our political differences, Mike is a little more likely to bring them up than I am. Perhaps it's because he's occasionally curious about where my liberal orientation comes from, aside from me just being a dumb writer.

Once, I gave him the simple explanation that I sometimes give to other conservatives who ask: I graduated from college in Ohio and moved to Chicago without a set political affiliation. But I rode the Lake Street El train every day past the hulking, haunting, and thankfully long since demolished Henry Horner Homes housing project on the West

Side while reading Alex Kotlowitz's then best seller *There Are No Children Here*, which is about life in that horrible place. And I decided that poverty was the biggest shame in America, the first thing we ought to try to fix. And though obviously neither political party was solving it, at least one of the parties occasionally spoke of poverty in ways that didn't seem to blame the parents of those poor kids down there at Henry Horner for being poor. So I became a Democrat and I've stayed one.

Mike accepted that, and we didn't need to wearily debate conservative or liberal approaches to welfare or the minimum wage, which would have led me to tell him about the more radical phases of my political journey— such as that rip-roaring trip through Red China in my mid-thirties with a gang of socialists. Maybe those socialists, whose ideas influence me to this day, think I should try to enlighten Mike on a few things. Perhaps Mike's suburban neighbors wonder how he could work for a Lyft-liberal like me. And maybe someday Mike and I will find ourselves on a long trip somewhere, and we'll get into it deeper.

But it sure doesn't seem urgent to either of us. Because I show up for work every day too. And I do what I say I'm going to do. I listen to his ideas. I consider his advice. I thank him for his help. And I pay him on time, every time.

We're both old enough that we don't take that stuff for granted.

Working with people, it seems to me, is the most reliable way to know what they are really made of—and to remember that on an assembly line, in a working mine, or on a tight deadline, your political orientation is (still) as good as mine.

If we're going to reach across, one place we'll do it is over a workbench.

VI.

FIRST,
DO NO HARM:
COMMUNICATING
WITH ACQUAINTANCES
AND STRANGERS

When you accidentally insult someone, you are embarrassed. You made a joke about how stupid church is *and Grandma was standing right behind you.* Luckily, it was *only* Grandma whom you upset with your careless remark. She knows you and loves you, and she knows you love her. You told her you were sorry, and she could see by your red face that you really were, and she forgave you. At no point did it occur to you to call Grandma a "snowflake," or to compose a screed about how easily offended some church people have become these days.

Now, thanks to social media, even the less influential among us can insult hundreds of people all at once—on purpose or by accident—sometimes without ever knowing we did.

We're doing it all the time, and we should be more careful.

Some of these accidents are mere mental lapses, like when I run across some deliciously nasty, dismissive, one-sided political insult and share it on social media, hoping that my six hundred Facebook friends who agree with it will see it, and thinking (magically) that the 241 who don't agree with it won't. Yes, we all live in our social media bubble—but everyone can hear right through them and see right through them, and they pop all the time.

Was making your tribe cackle at a meme on a Saturday morning worth making the other tribe pile on more sandbags and cock their rifles?

Other accidental insults are the result of our inherent human clumsiness. When we knock things over in real life, we gasp in horror. We say we're sorry. And we scramble to help clean up the mess. But when we shit the bed on social media, we're less apologetic. In fact, our first reaction is to deny we broke anything at all—or to say, *If you didn't want us to spill your precious, delicate glass of milk, you shouldn't have left it on the counter.*

Americans who think we have any part at all in making a less chaotic and angry society will take greater care not to break other people's things—and when we inevitably do, we will apologize and try to make amends.

Privileged Is a Fighting Word

M y classmates at Hudson High School celebrated our thirty-year reunion awhile ago. I did not attend, because high school memories are for me approximately three-quarters bad and one-quarter blank. My only contribution to the Ohio proceedings was to remark on Facebook, from Chicago, that the reason I didn't go was that the school's culture was characterized by "WASPy, insulated arrogance."

It was just the kind of rhetorical punch bowl turd that I'm trying as hard as I can to keep from dropping at this moment when Americans don't need more reasons to despise each other or distrust their punch.

I did, however, consciously restrain myself from also calling my old schoolmates "privileged." Because that, as we know, is a *real* fighting word.

No person should ever call another person "privileged"—at least, not if the person is truly trying to communicate. Why? Because no matter how advantaged a person may be thanks to his or her social class, race, gender, physique, nation of origin, region of origin, city of origin, neighborhood of origin, or block of origin—no one ever *feels* privileged.

That's because even the most privileged person had an alcoholic mother and teenage acne. And now has adult psoriasis, a permanent case of impostor syndrome, panic attacks, weight issues, relationship issues, gambling issues—or all of the above.

And on a day-to-day basis, everyone—even the most gifted of us—feels that he or she has fought like a dog to get to cocktail hour: has climbed out of a warm bed in the cold dark, beaten traffic, tolerated crazy coworkers, sated bottomless customers, and slogged through yet more traffic home while on the phone with a narcissistic relative, only to be told upon walking in the back door that the fucking dishwasher is leaking badly.

At what point in that day is that person open—even if it's a white male Yale grad, and the traffic is three more Lear jets ahead of him on the corporate strip, and his crazy coworker is Mark Zuckerberg, and the dishwasher is on his yacht—to being called "privileged"?

Privileged is a term for the academy. It's for general discussion. When it comes to personal conversation, it's purely a fighting word. If you're trying to communicate with live people, you're better off criticizing them for something they can do something about. And "check your privilege" doesn't count as something a person can actually do, because if that were actually possible, "privilege" wouldn't be such a big deal.

Let us be clear: There is white privilege. There is male privilege. There is class privilege. But it's a sociological term, not a psychological one. It's for essays, not for communication with a real, live person. It's true—just not inside you.

I'm a runner, and the repetitive mindlessness of this sorry hobby gives me a chance to think about privilege daily, in terms of the best metaphor I know: When I'm running *against* the wind, I curse every gust. I'm outraged at the god who made the glaciers that plowed this frozen Chicago prairie by the lake. So you'd think that when I turn around and begin running *with* the wind, I'd feel pushed along and grateful for it.

Nope. You know what it feels like to run with the wind? It feels like no wind at all. And I don't feel gratitude, either, because I'm still having to run, still getting tired, still sweating, still drooling snot out my nose, and still bored out of my middle-aged mind whenever I'm not stewing about my middle-aged problems.

And if I ever wheezed into the back door bragging about the eight miles I just covered, and my no-account wife said, "Yeah, but the prevailing wind was at your back"—that meteorological observation would not be welcomed. But of course, she would never say that, because who would?

Privilege is real. But don't expect anybody to feel regularly and truly grateful for having it—or gracious toward you when you point it out.

Why We Don't Like Environmental Nags,
Even Though They're Right

Everyone's sitting around talking about the economy, or the gun problem, or the homelessness problem, or LGBTQ rights, or the Middle East, or concussions in the NFL, and suddenly you realize that *one* person hasn't been heard from in a while.

And the reason she hasn't been heard from is because she's *about* to be heard from.

She's been leaning back slightly, so nobody can see she is holding a royal flush. She's been waiting for just the right moment to lay it down.

"Of course none of this really matters," she says at last, taking a sip of her brandy without really looking up. "Because the real problem is climate change."

Just because she's right, that doesn't make it polite—or productive, or even honest—for her to say it.

It's not fair game for a spouse to end an argument over squeezing the toothpaste tube by referring to the time, ten years ago, when the other spouse was caught in bed with the neighbor lady. Nor would you congratulate a person on a job promotion by recalling the day you won your Pulitzer Prize. And you don't put a conversation about the latest mass shooting in a mall into perspective by saying it's not as bad as Hitler killing six million Jews.

Here's how polite *I* am: when the environmental nag plays the global warming card, I refrain from expressing my feeling that the real problem isn't global warming. As I learned in third grade (and it started a nihilist streak in me), the sun is going to go out in about five billion years anyway, and humanity is going to disappear into the darkness, no matter what the water levels are at the time. Five billion years, one hundred years—what difference does it make to you and me?

Look, if I were privileged enough to muse about nature all day, I'd be frustrated too. But like most people, I'm sort of busy with trivial concerns like providing for my family and hunting and gathering for a little enjoyment in life. I guess I'm failing to hug the forest for the trees.

We're all going to die anyway in the end, so who cares whether it's by drowning or freezing?

(You see how it feels?)

Ghosting Is a Crime Against Humanity

Some crimes receive too much punishment, and other crimes don't receive enough. For instance, every boozer knows that hungover driving is twice as dangerous as buzzed driving, yet it's perfectly legal. And you can lose your livelihood for making an unwanted pass at a colleague, but on the flip side, you can "ghost" someone you said you cared about, and no one can hold you accountable.

Ghosting is a new word, but not a new concept. Growing up, we all heard stories of kids whose parents (usually fathers) disappeared or "ran off." And long before Tinder, ghosting was described in the lyrics of "50 Ways to Leave Your Lover," with Paul Simon advising, "Slip out the back, Jack."

It was how I resigned my first job in Chicago—near the end of my first week as the "night waterman" at a public golf course. After four endless midnight-to-eight shifts with a deranged Vietnam veteran as my only companion, I simply turned off the alarm on the fifth night and didn't go in. I remember writhing in my bed as I listened over the answering machine to the voice of the disappointed superintendent, who had hired me (and paid for my drug test) earlier that same week. He said he'd send my check in the mail.

I only had to feel that way once to realize I would never do that to anyone—boss, friend, lover, or even enemy—ever again. I think breaking off a relationship without telling why, or saying goodbye, is one of the most violent things a person can do to another person.

And yet it's become a near standard practice in online dating, where people see one another, first, as profiles; second, as sex partners; and only third, on the off chance that things happen to go really well, as people. A dear friend of mine got ghosted not long ago, and it made me feel just about the same way I'd feel if the bastard had hit her. Not just protective of her, but protective of *us*—people with a conscience who are supposed to be doing what Kurt Vonnegut said we were all put here to do: "Help each other through this thing, whatever it is."

If you feel strongly enough to break off a relationship—or quit a job, or resign a client, or end any significant partnership—you should explain why you've done it. I believe it's something close to a Law of Communication. You should explain so the other person can learn something from hearing you say it, and so you can learn from hearing yourself say it. And you should explain so you don't leave the other person more generally cynical and lonely, despairing over the unreliability of other people and the lack of goodness in the world, you nihilistic, cowardly, no-account creep.

Littering is against the law. Harassment is against the law. Reckless endangerment is against the law. Torture is against the law. Fraud is against the law. Ghosting should be against the law.

It's Called "Decorum," and
It's Not the Worst Thing in the World

I once told my five-year-old daughter that in our family, we don't say *passed away*—we say *died*. The next morning, she asked me what I was doing on the couch. I told her I was snoozing. "In this family," she said, "we don't say 'snoozing.' We say 'sleeping.'"

Around writers and editors like me, who fancy ourselves clear-eyed intellectuals, the word *euphemism* has a bad reputation. Euphemism obfuscates, and obfuscation is bad because reality is good and we're tough and we can take it.

But in this hard American moment, I'm seeing more and more virtue in the occasional soft word.

There's a cooler of beer in the entrance to the local grocery store. Now, I might be inclined to have a beer at the store—and I like a hoppy daytime beer as much as the next hipster—but I've been discouraged by the advertisement that hangs above the cooler:

DRINK WHILE YOU SHOP.

Drink while you shop? Surely we can take the edge off that. How about *Refresh yourself while you replenish your pantry,* or *Have a brew while you browse?* Or something!

Young people in particular—taut muscles and tough meat—overlook the social and psychological need for the occasional lingo-softener. I tried to check in early to a hotel in Wisconsin once, and the young woman behind the desk said I couldn't yet. Her reason: "Your room is still dirty."

Dirty!

I later learned that's backstage hotel industry jargon—like the inelegant catering term *heavy hors d'oeuvres* that we're now seeing emblazoned in calligraphy on high society invitations. *Why?*

To attendees of his conferences, my old boss Larry Ragan gave a lunch on the first day only. On the second day, his brochures advised, "Enjoy lunch on your own." Isn't that better for everyone involved than *No lunch today?*

As we do with "white lies," it seems to me we ought to come up with a separate term for the socially useful euphemism. The "usephemism," perhaps.

In business correspondence with Europeans lately, I enjoy what I call "Europhemisms." When you invite an American communicator to a conference, he might decline because *They cut our budget* or *My boss doesn't let us travel for conferences.* Yet in many years of inviting and being invited by Europeans to attend and speak at conferences, I've never heard about a budget—do they even have them over there?—and I very rarely hear directly about the person's boss. Much more common is the sort of language I heard from a German speechwriter the other day, whom I'd invited to come to an event here: "I spoke to my colleagues," she wrote, "and they gave me the go-ahead."

In this case, is *colleagues* a politeness meaning "boss"? I imagine so, but I don't need to know for sure. Nor do I want to! I want to go on thinking that this speechwriter and her colleagues gather periodically to discuss the relative merits and costs of one another's professional and personal desires, weigh them against everyone else's needs and wishes, and come to a thoughtful decision that's best for every individual and the organization as whole!

Assuming *colleagues* is indeed a euphemism for "boss," I respect the dual impulse: to insulate me from the vulgar and petty and ultimately irrelevant machinations of her communication department, and also to protect the institution she works for from making an undeserved poor first impression on an American conference producer who has no call to judge.

I've argued throughout my whole communication career for candor and against pretense. But I must admit, I do appreciate a bit of social grace every now and again.

There's an old joke about a newly appointed drill sergeant who calls the company together to announce, "Private Murphy, your grandfather died!" Murphy bursts into tears in front of all his mates, and then runs off to hide in the barracks in shame. The drill sergeant is called on the carpet by the commanding officer, who tells him, for God's sake, to be more tactful next time. So the next time the drill sergeant has some bad news to report, he calls the company together again. This time he shouts, "Everybody whose mother didn't die last night, step forward. Not so fast, Anderson!"

Speaking of Decorum,
Did You Know Chicago Has Three Streets
That Rhyme with *Vagina*?*

I have a complicated relationship with swearing. Because swearing is a complicated thing.

I never used the word *douche* until the past few years. My college roommate used it, and I thought it sounded mean and misogynistic. I still wouldn't call a woman a douche, but when it became popular to call a man a douche—and to describe him and his douchebaggery as "douchey"—I got on board the bagwagon.

I don't like the idea of calling a woman a cunt, either. But I just delight in calling cunty men cunts. It's also fun to call a woman a dick.

And that's one of the big things about swearing: it's fun.

It was a woman who got me interested in swearing in the first place: my mother. When I was five years old and supposed to be asleep in another room, I heard her talking to my dad and casually referring to an acquaintance of theirs as an asshole. I began to giggle uncontrollably at the hilarious rudeness of rhetorically reducing one of God's magnificent creatures to a dark orifice an inch or two in dirty diameter. I remember thinking, quite literally: *This swearing—it's for me, from now on.*

Mom was a mentor in this area. She thought my father was a prig.

When Dad was out of town on business trips, she would set the oven timer and let my little sister and me say anything we wanted for an hour. When we ran out of ideas, she helped us, with inventive terms like *double-decker pecker wrecker*, and the complete sentence allegedly spoken by a World War I ambulance driver, explaining to his sergeant that his rig broke down: "The fuckin' fucker's fucked."

An old writer friend once asked me, "If you say *shit* in front of a lady, then what do you say when you have a flat tire on the Brooklyn Bridge?" I puzzled on this for years, until I realized, *You say* shit *again!*

I swore in front of my daughter all the time when she was little, though I didn't allow her to say *crap* in the house because when I hear that word, I think of the real thing. I also forbade her to say *cuss*, which sounds to my sensitive ears too much like *pus*.

Now she's seventeen and tells me she swears all the time with her friends, but she never swears in front of me or my wife or any other adults (or little kids), because she agrees that random strangers shouldn't have to hear you swearing at the top of your fucking lungs.

Swearing is freedom. Still, let's try not to upset random strangers and casual acquaintances gratuitously and unnecessarily, like I just did.

*Paulina, Melvina, and Lunt.

A Handshake Means
Never Having to Text *I'm Sorry* ☹

An unsatisfying interaction with a construction worker reminded me of how dependent I have become on email and other electronic communication to smooth over, round out, sand down, and shine up many sloppy, distracted, thoughtless in-person communications.

Stanley, with his fingers splayed on each hand like a damaged asterisk, worked in our home on and off for most of a year. He remodeled our kitchen, built my home office, and renovated our daughter's bedroom. He was Polish, and at first I didn't understand much of what he said. But so enthusiastically did he try to say it, that I tried too—mostly only pretending to comprehend his juggling of a terribly limited English vocabulary. Whether he was trying to tell me about the new refrigerator or his family's immigration to the United States, Stanley's English diction consisted primarily of different combinations of "*Not problem*" and "*Ess connected*" and "*I like*" and "*Ess OK.*"

Nevertheless, it seemed as if his English improved over the months he was here. Then again, he'd been in the United States a long time, and it's unlikely that he made such great strides all of a sudden, so it's more likely that my listening was improving. Meanwhile, Stanley and his taciturn partner Tony worked like steam engines for a not-so-extravagant wage. So the language barrier—not problem.

Stanley was a good sport whenever the dog got loose and ran into their construction scene. "I like dog!" he would shout. "Ess OK! I like him!" He was warm to our daughter and unfailingly good-humored with all of us, even when you could tell his sixty-year-old body was tired. He even did a couple of completely extra things, like fixing a leaky toilet and carrying our heavy window air conditioners down to the basement.

So when he finished the kitchen only a few days after the deadline, and as Christmas approached, I wanted to thank him for more than the work he'd done. I wanted to thank him for the way he'd done it. So I bought him a big handle of Sobieski vodka. I bought Tony one too.

But when I went to hand it to Stanley, I kind of panicked. And when he turned to leave, I suddenly felt sure I hadn't steadily looked him in the eye while I thanked him and wished him a Merry Christmas. I realized I hadn't even shaken his craggy hand—which I had done at a number of congratulatory junctures before!

As he walked out the door, I felt a pang of agony. In my mind, my body language had conveyed exactly the opposite of what I'd wanted it to convey. I was afraid I had told him: *Thanks for building my house. Now take your vodka and get out of here.*

And then a familiar, comforting thought came: *I'll send Stanley a little note, conveying my gratitude in writing, using my special writer's words!*

But Stanley doesn't do email. If you saw his fingers, you would know this. More to the point, Stanley doesn't do little notes of any kind. Again, the fingers, and the English. Stanley does handshakes, eye contact, smiling, and laughing. And I hadn't done enough of any of that on my last chance to say goodbye to him before Christmas and the end of our time together.

It seems to me we all ought to concentrate more on communicating better on the first try—in real time, in real life, with all the people in our lives—rather than relying on emailed thank-you notes and Facebook pokes to clean up our thoughtless mistakes and omissions.

They don't work as well as the real thing anyway.

"Sniper, Take Out the Subject": Killing the Conversational Assassin Within Us All

I call it Irish Communication, but that's just because I think of myself as Irish. It really should just be called "civilized communication." Most of us know how this style of communicating works, because most of us do it every day. Then there are the Conversational Assassins . . .

But first, Irish Communication: You and your conversation partner say stuff back and forth, looking for points of agreement over which the two of you can bond. Then you use that plateau of agreement to launch into a new topic, on which you both *continue* to seek cozy points of common interest and shared sentiment.

Say Seattle comes up for some reason, and I explain that I became fascinated by that city at a young age because I liked the Seattle Seahawks. As a kid, I was a big fan of their quarterback Jim Zorn, and now I love their cool, modern uniforms.

Now, suppose you hate Seattle, hate the Seahawks, hate their uniforms, and barely remember Zorn. Here's what you say, Irish style: you say, "Zorn! Wasn't he a scrappy little left-hander?"

And I say, "Yes! He was tiny, and they were a mediocre team, and he carried them on his shoulders during those years."

And then you talk about *your* favorite underdog team. And speaking of underdogs, you ask if I've ever heard your theory about how to make steady money betting on underdog baseball teams that are playing at home . . . And so on and so forth.

The two of us keep doing this back-and-forth until we find something really meaningful to talk about—or we run out of things we care to discuss—or one of us says something so preposterous or monstrous that the other is morally compelled to beat him over the head with a folding chair. Whichever comes first.

Usually, if you and the other person practice this kind of civilized communication for long enough, you both find yourselves drunk on beer or high on coffee (or life!) and feeling better for having turned a stranger into an acquaintance. You've just made your world a little warmer.

Irish Communication comes so naturally to me—and to most of us, really—that it can be hard to see it as an actual technique. Until you run into a person, as you occasionally do, who practices its very opposite: Conversational Assassination.

I have at least a few Conversational Assassins in my life. They are actually warm and caring people, big smilers, and easy huggers—and bright! But talking to them is utterly horrible, because they are the exact opposite of Irish Communicators.

Instead of automatically searching their conversation partner's utterings for commonality, Conversational Assassins zero in on the smallest difference. So if I say I like Seattle, I like the Seahawks, I like Jim Zorn, and I like the modern uniforms—and the Assassin also loves the Seahawks, Seattle, and Zorn—the Assassin will respond by saying, "Oh, those new uniforms are the absolute worst! How can you like them?"

So I'll change the subject. I'll mention that I won a free Caribbean vacation, all expenses paid, to a little resort where everybody has their own private cabana and free booze all day!

"What's the food like?" will come the response. "Did you look into that? Because I went to a resort in the Caribbean once, and the food was just terrible."

That's a stone-cold Conversational Assassin.

I've studied these people. I've even dared to confront them about their homicidal tendencies. When I have, the response is inevitably, "That's what I love about you. You don't mind a good argument."

Well, yes, John Wilkes Booth/Lee Harvey Oswald/James Earl Ray—but I don't consider frozen yogurt flavors a suitable subject for a kitchen-clearing conversational donnybrook.

Conversational Assassins are not terrible people. They're just terrible people to talk to, because they gravitate toward disagreement, like moths to a flaming asshole.

Like a lot of Americans, these days.

Don't be one of them.

Do You Tell Stories
to Connect with People or
to Keep Them Away?

Spend ten minutes at a happy hour with professional writers and public relations people, and someone will bring up storytelling, as if it's a wholly novel communication magic trick that transforms every human interaction into a spellbinding, life-changing emotional adventure.

These people haven't met my sailing mate.

Some years ago I had the good fortune to be invited on a macho errand: helping my brother-in-law sail his big boat across a fat stretch of the Atlantic Ocean, from Baltimore to the Virgin Islands. I also had the disastrous bad fortune of having as my night watchmate a guy whom we'll call Frank, just in case. But really, the guy is so deeply oblivious to the world around him that there is absolutely no chance he will ever hear of my telling this story.

A little background: On a long-distance trip, you obviously sail through the nights, too, and someone on the boat needs to keep watch at all times. So the captain assigns shifts, and everyone usually gets a partner, because it's easier to stay awake in the heaving blackness when you have someone else to talk to.

We had only four people on this trip, and one was my brother-in-law's daughter. She couldn't stand Frank, so she lobbied to be her dad's watchmate, claiming with a cunning smile that she wanted "quality time" with her dad.

So I got Frank. Every night from midnight to five, just me and Frank. To say Frank was a difficult watch mate is to fail to say he was a challenge to my philosophical understanding of the meaning and purpose of human interaction.

Frank was a radio station that never went off the air, coming in over a radio that couldn't be turned down. He would unspool uninterrupted and uniformly empty yarns about his career as a fireman and his semi-retirement as a professional sailor; about his girlfriend in Mexico and his wife in California; about himself, himself, himself.

Never once did Frank express any curiosity about me or ask any question at all beyond those bogus kinds of queries designed to set up another interminable self-glorifying fable: *Have you ever found yourself at the edge of a raging forest fire with only a shovel in one hand and a pickaxe in the other? No? Well let me tell you . . .*

Every night at midnight I had to rise from my bunk and step up into the dark, chilly cockpit for five more hours, all by myself—just me alongside Frank's narcissism, shallowness, uneducated smugness, phony bravado, questionable morality, and sheer boringness!

It wasn't that Frank was painful to deal with. It was that he was an affront to everything my dear, departed parents had told me to value in human beings: curiosity, humor, depth, candor. It was as if my divorced, deceased parents in heaven had set aside their differences for long enough to get together and search the world for the one perfect asshole. They had found Frank and arranged for me to share night duty with him, just as a test of fealty to them! There were moments when I felt that if I didn't throw Frank overboard—or leap into the inky, cold ocean myself—I was being disloyal to my parents' memory.

For nine days and nine nights, Frank must have told me ten thousand stories, all of which added up to exactly nothing. They were so much patter, designed to fill dead air with words that made their speaker appear the way he hoped his audience would see him: calm and knowing and capable, humble and brave and wise.

Of those ten thousand stories, I can't remember a single one. Instead, I remember those nights I spent alone with Frank—a total of forty-five hours in the windy black—as one endless, living death, a waking coma from which I was lucky to emerge with most of my faculties.

And yet in a magazine article that I wrote about the trip, I described Frank as "loquacious."

I wrote: "Night watches put a premium on a skill that's rare in this day and age: a person's ability to make a short story long. Frank is the Michael Jordan of that skill."

Now, how did I come to like Frank well enough to be able to write about him graciously—and even remember him fondly? It was not a gradual process, but a result that came about all of a sudden—with one story that Frank told me on the last night of the trip.

It wasn't much of a story. In fact, it was probably the shortest story he told the whole trip. And he didn't exactly tell it to me as much as he sort of divulged it. In fact, he kind of coughed it up.

Frank's older brother, whom he idolized and adored and modeled himself after—and who had loved him and watched out for him while growing up, taking the place of a father who wasn't there—was killed in a car accident when Frank was about thirteen.

What?

I was just hearing now, after nine straight nights of long-form inanities, about what must have been the single most formative moment of Frank's life. And as I was hearing it, told in a quiet, honest, true way—in the middle of the night, in the middle of the ocean—I could see Frank's face in the faint glow of the electronic compass. Even behind his mustache, it was the face of a thirteen-year-old boy.

After a silence, I considered how to express that I understood Frank's brother's death must have been devastating. In fact, I was already beginning to understand that such a death might be so catastrophic and soul-tearing as to cause a human being to turn into a twenty-four-hour broadcasting radio station up in a tall tower with a razor-wire fence around it.

"I can't imagine how crushing that must have been," I said.

"Yeah," he said quietly. "It was real hard on my mom."

And with that story (Story Number 10,001), Frank was utterly and forever transformed in my mind. He went from an example of something—a type of something, a hologram to be shown to other people as something to be avoided—into a human being.

When a person is transformed in that way, you don't have to like him, of course—I never sailed with Frank again—but you do have to respect him and acknowledge him as a fellow traveler. And if you say you love human beings, you have to love this one, too.

VII.

WANTING
AND BELOVED:
COMMUNICATING WITH
OUR FAMILIES
AND OUR FRIENDS

B y now you've noticed that this book has migrated from the philosophical to the professional to the political to the social toward
the personal. As we enter the realm of our intimate relationships, things
become at once more specific and more ethereal. And any wisdom is
better conveyed in poetry than prose—in brief observations and shared
impressions rather than artfully reasoned and well-supported essays—
because that's the way we actually communicate with our intimates.

When I'm teaching writers how to become speechwriters, I tell them
they need to focus on the difference between an audience's patience for a
long speech on a grand topic versus a family's patience. A speaker might
stand before the National Press Club and ask the audience to be seated,
tell them why "I called you all together this morning," and inform them,
"Today I want to talk to you about three things . . ." But if you come home
from that speech, and your spouse or lover or son or daughter bothers to
ask you what the speech was about, and you open by telling them "the
speech was about three things," you'll find yourself reciting those three
things to yourself.

Like characters in good books or movies, families and friends don't
communicate with one another in composed prose. It's all action. Even
the words we use—the movie characters' dialogue—are action. And it's
almost all improvised.

But inside this infinite fast-and-loose, direct-and-indirect communication that goes on in families and among friends, a few universal principles are worth trying to keep in mind.

Marital Communication
Is Wiping Your Eyes in a Monsoon

real conversation with my wife of twenty-five years:

"You know," she says brightly, "I'm not mad at all that you've planned a motorcycle trip right before our family vacation."
"You're not?"
"No. But *you* would be *so* mad if I did something like that."
"I would?"
"Oh yeah. *So mad.*"
"It sounds like you are mad that I would be mad if you did something like this."
"Yes, I guess I am."
"So you're mad at something the hypothetical me would hypothetically feel toward the hypothetical you."
"Yes."
"Seems like it might just be easier to be mad at me for the real thing, doesn't it?"
"Yeah, I guess that's right."

Cue grim laughter.

I've said in a hundred ways that I think communication is acts as much as words. In a marriage, that goes double—especially in a long marriage like mine. There have been one or two troubled times when it has occurred to me out of desperation to begin a written dialogue with my wife. Maybe I could get my thoughts across in cool, rational, accurate words before the thing escalated into a noisy fight or hot tears.

But I've never gotten more than four sentences in before deleting the email. Even for a writer, the idea of using words to parse out the problems and unhappiness and confusion that arise in a relationship this close and this long—it feels like a master mechanic trying to do brain surgery with a socket set, or a brain surgeon trying to pull an engine with a scalpel. It's hopeless.

Like any long and close relationship between human beings, a marriage is an endless series of deals that no bar association could codify—a million-page binding document with so many obscure precedents and antecedents, stipulations, contingency clauses, and rights of first and last refusal that the only way to sum it up is by saying or demonstrating *I love you* or *I hate you* or *I don't care one way or the other anymore*. You've heard of a no-fault divorce? The alternative is what the rest of us have: an everybody's-fault marriage.

A marriage is also a sequence of photographs you never got developed: a collection of memories misremembered by only the two of you. Like that time you were in Venice and saw another couple reading a book together, with her tearing out a page when she was finished and handing it to him, except your spouse insists that was in Cuyahoga Falls, Ohio.

The term *fake news* almost certainly was invented by a wife, to combat her husband's habitual hyperbolizing. She salts his words before she even tastes them.

Meanwhile, he realized long ago that his wedding vows aren't promissory as much as they're journalistic: he *is* only as rich or poor, sick or healthy, happy or unhappy as she is. If they are having a hard time, his golf handicap goes up.

A marriage is both touches and touches withheld, both glances and averted eyes. It's a regular temperature check. *Did you sleep well? What are you thinking for dinner tonight?* and *What should we get your mom for her birthday?*

So what exactly would I tell my wife in an email? What would I say that she doesn't already know so much more subtly than my poor words can ever express? The act of sending the email would tell her so much more than the contents ever could. It would tell her I am desperate. (And she probably already knows that, too.)

We went to a marriage counselor once. Our mutual decision to go told each of us more about the marriage—the trouble it was in, and also our mutual commitment to carry on—than anything we said or heard in there.

Long ago, my dad wrote:

> A love made well to begin with is much like a silver chalice that is made well to begin with. The years don't, in any way, diminish its capacity. Time cannot tarnish it beyond what a gentle touch can wipe away in a moment. A single flower brought to it for no real reason on a rainy day can brighten it almost beyond belief.

When I got married in 1994, everybody in the office signed a card. *Stay together thirty years,* scrawled the crusty old publisher. *Then you'll know what love is.*

Now that my wife and I are getting there, I can tell you: marriage is staying together long enough to know what love is—until you know it so well, you aren't able to put it into words.

Words Hold People Together

When my dad was dying of pancreatic cancer in the dark American winter of 2008, I kept a journal. Here's one entry:

Dad can't write anymore because the pills make his head fuzzy. He wants me to come up with something to write back to "all these people," a half-dozen family members and friends who have written him letters telling him what he's meant to them.

I instinctively resist because I think writers can't ghost-write for writers, a notion he seems to think is a cop-out. "I asked David for help writing these letters," I hear him telling my sister on the phone, "and he put on his hat and went out the door."

So I try.

I tell him he's already done his part in the lives of these letter writers, and all they really want to know is that he received their letters of appreciation. *Thank you for your fine letter*, I propose he writes on cards that I'll address. *And I want you to know that it meant a great deal to me, and so do you.*

"But that's what *you'd* write," he says angrily. "It's not what *I'd* write!"

Between reruns of the above episode, words hold us together.

He half-remembers a fragment from a poem he once knew: *like a bubble it burst, all at once and nothing first.* We spend time searching the internet in vain for the rest of the poem.

We make fun of the hospice nurse, who can't pronounce a particular one-syllable local street name correctly because of her Southern accent.

At the dinner table, he stares at a photograph of himself in the cockpit of an airplane that has the number *N1451R* on the fuselage. "Five-One Ringo," he says over and over and over and over because doing so makes him feel like a pilot again.

Reading the latest issue of *Old Cars Weekly*, he grumbles about the term "swapped out" as it's used to refer to engines that are replaced with other engines. The "out" part, he says, is "totally unnecessary." He says so with such increasing force that I'm compelled to remind him, defensively, that I didn't invent the term. *"Well, you need to do something about it!"*

Words to us are things, every bit as much as airplanes and automobiles and oxycodone pills are things, and we hold onto them, one of us on each end, and we spin around together.

And here's another entry, from a month later:

I told my sisters in an email yesterday, "I have to find something to tell people who ask me how Dad's funeral was besides, 'It was great!'"

I suppose I should first answer for myself what *was* so great about the funeral, and the days surrounding it.

I think a funeral has more potential than any other kind of an occasion to bond people together. And especially a certain kind of funeral. Like my Dad's funeral.

It was a day of *communication.*

Everyone who attended this funeral had a common cause. We were in Middletown, Ohio, in the middle of the bitter winter to mourn what we all agreed was a significant loss. No one came passive-aggressively, as many do to family holidays. No one came looking to get laid, as some do to weddings. And no one secretly suspected the transformation we were acknowledging was a temporary one, as many also do at weddings.

The occasion was so undeniably real—a human being had gone from breathing to not breathing, from flesh to ashes—that no one talked incessantly about the wonders of the latest iPod. Intra-family agendas and rivalries were lint on a black suit. Even conversations about Obama's crucial economic agenda—even these sounded tinny against the great big backdrop of the death of our personal FDR, Truman, Eisenhower, and Kennedy, just to name the first few.

Bluster was out; vulnerability was in. I'm not somebody who believes the more you cry, the psychically healthier you are. Still, it seems good to have an interaction once in a while—or a hundred interactions in one week—where somebody says, "I am sorry you are sad," and you aren't compelled to say anything more than, "Thank you." Human beings deny their frailty and their pain for very good, practical reasons: they don't want to be a burden to their friends, and they don't want to show their underbelly to their enemies. A funeral gives us a chance to remove the mask, and I'm glad I had the courage, and the trust in my friends and family, to take that chance this week.

The subject of the funeral was an enthusiastic person who had integrity. However complex a character my dad was (and he was!), and whatever different things he meant to thousands of different people over his eighty-five years, we were still all talking about the same fellow. Didn't matter if it was his boyhood friend Bill from the 1920s; his girlfriend Louise from 1940; his nephew Tad, who was a "Tadpole" in the 1950s; his first set of kids, who came of age in the 1960s; his second set, who grew up in the 1970s; or my daughter, who met Granddaddy in 2003—we were all talking about the fellow who jumped out of bed every morning, the kidder whom you could kid, the whistler, the builder of elaborate model train layouts in his basement who believed they were real. The word guy, the shy guy—all those things. And the stories held together. The colors all matched. It takes a human being—a certain kind of human being—to unify dozens and dozens of people in a spirit as concentrated as the one that healed me in Middletown last week.

A reacquaintance, not with one or two things "that really matter," but with the incredible range of things that matter. I cried while reading some of my dad's words at the funeral, and two days later when I smelled the sleeve of a plaid flannel shirt hanging in his closet, I fell on the floor and howled. What exists in between the words and the scents of the people in our lives? Everything does.

So I spent a week with most of the people that I love— after exchanging tender phone calls and emails with the rest of the people that I love—talking about everything that matters and nothing that doesn't matter.

How was my dad's funeral?

It was great.

It's Easy to Communicate with
Your Kids—at First

When kids are little, they ask cute questions that are easy to answer. "Is it OK not to believe in skeletons?" my daughter asked me when she was three.

Also: "Could a coconut kill you?"

"Why don't motorcycles have seatbelts?"

One time after a shirtless, muscle-bound Black jogger ran past us on the sidewalk: "Dad, do white people ever have muscles?"

Riding past a Chicago cemetery, she saw that some grave markers were taller than others. "Dad, were those people bigger than everybody else?"

When she was about eight, I was telling her how to dispose of her tray at a local cafeteria. "Dad, this isn't my first rodeo," she said. "Wait. What is a rodeo?"

And now she's seventeen, and I'm the one asking all the questions: *Do you have homework? Who's going to the party? Are the parents going to be there? What time will you be home?*

I asked her a good question one Saturday morning at breakfast, when she was trying and really failing to tell me why she'd been feeling unhappy lately. I heard myself suggesting, "Could it be you've discovered that life is meaningless and people are monsters?"

She looked at me with the wounded astonishment of someone who has had their worst fears confirmed.

I spent the rest of the meal mouthing words I don't remember about how people are also beautiful, and how we must make our lives meaningful. Child development specialists will have to forgive me, for this *is* my first rodeo.

Another Saturday, I picked her up from a sleepover way up on the North Side. She had her learner's permit, and she was driving us home, down Western Avenue. She was tired, and we were quiet. And suddenly it popped into my head to say, "You know, don't you, that I love you just as much now that you're a complicated teenager as I did when you were a simple, pure-hearted little kid?"

She said, "That can't possibly be."

And after I nodded that it was true indeed, she looked through the windshield into the middle distance, trying to fathom how.

That was better, right?

Communication Works Best in Large Doses

Y ou hear all the time about people who are good to be with . . . in small doses.

But honestly, most of the people I know—me included, I think—are actually better in large doses. With a little more time to move around in, we're less noisy and opinionated. More reflective. More relaxed. More honest. Better listeners. More able to focus on the few things that matter, and less distracted by the avalanches of shit that don't. More liable to laugh like a little kid.

More ourselves.

I took a road trip with my old writer pal Paul a few years ago. Actually, it's been most of a decade now, but I remember it so well.

On a four-day round trip from Chicago, we saw my boyhood home in Ohio and his boyhood home in New Jersey. We stayed at the Jane Hotel in New York and went to McSorley's Old Ale House and stumbled into a big Wall Street protest. We attended a wedding at an opulent but rain-washed horse farm in Connecticut.

In between, it was just the dull, gray, hypnotic highway ahead, and all that time to talk. Dozens and dozens of hours, to talk and talk and talk . . .

I'd forgotten what happens on a car trip that long.

The adrenaline wears off by the second day, and your conversations take on an unfamiliar rhythm. Their properties change. Their purpose changes, and then the talk sheds all purposes, except for passing the time. *Long stories short? No, short stories long!*

You stop trying to justify the stories you are telling as being apropos of something. Instead, it's: *Hey, this just popped into my head, so I'm gonna tell it to you.*

Occasionally a decision must be made. *Should we get something to eat here, or wait until we have to get gas?* On a long trip, you dispense with chivalry and you wordlessly settle on a reliable system: You impose your will when it is strong. Otherwise, you do what the other guy suggests until you decide he is gravely wrong.

And as you cruise the last few hours home in gathering quiet, you begin to realize that a four-day conversation between two friends amounts to a kind of Constitution As Far As We're Concerned. Nothing that you'd ever try to get anyone else to sign—but something set down in words, and stored where you can get at it, in the cloud.

Do you have a good friend you've never had a road trip with?

Find a reason. I'm glad I did.

Stay Away from People Who Hate You, Even if They Love You, Too

As I get older, the hard-and-fast rules that I applied to life as a young man have mostly been broken and forgotten. But the guidelines I follow now have been forged by experience, and they are becoming more and more useful. One of them is that I no longer spend time with people who feel contempt or envy or hatred for me—even if they like me or love me most of the time.

I once saw stormy relationships as a sign that I embraced the complexity of life. I now realize that life is complex enough when surrounded by friends and family who overlook my many faults instead of collecting and classifying them for the David Murray Is an Asshole Museum they are hoping to open someday. Breaking bread with people, even those I love, who fondle my shortcomings like their own genitals leads to perversion and degradation.

The question arises: *Do I deserve to be resented?* Probably by my enemies, if I have them—but not by my friends!

And of course, I resent *myself* plenty—though perhaps not as much as a colleague who once refused to attend his own performance review on the grounds that his supervisor couldn't possibly know just how slack and dishonest a worker he really was.

It's both inevitable and healthy that you'll have people in your life whom you disagree with, but you don't want people who despise you. You can surely smell the difference.

Get away, and watch the whole world brighten up.

Love Thy Neighbor (and Like Him, Too)

I t's dangerous to say it or even think it, but neighbors are important to a happy life. Why dangerous? Because you can't control who lives next door. Why important? Same reason. Your ability to make genuinely friendly relationships with the people who happen to live next door— that makes a real difference in your life. And even if your interactions are superficial, the relationship is not. You see each other every day, backstage, in every season, in every mood. Eventually, you get to know each other pretty well, whether you want to or not. So the difference between loving and hating the people living out their existence only a few feet and a little brick and plaster away from where you're living out yours—that also makes a huge difference in your spiritual condition.

I once avoided my neighbors, out of fear that they could ruin my life. I've learned to cultivate those relationships (carefully), to make my life better. As I tried to express in a 2011 blog post, a particular set of neighbors, all of us long moved away now, taught me how.

> I won't share this until I've had a chance to make sure it's logical and not banal and mostly spelled right, but I am writing it on Sunday morning from the mild but happy haze in the smack-middle of a boozy three-day July Fourth weekend, which has already seen a 4:00 a.m. bedtime, a cookout with the neighbors, and a night sleeping under the stars with my young daughter on her balcony. Ahead is an afternoon on a

friend's boat, followed by another all-day, building-wide cookout tomorrow amid the indescribable gunpowder ruckus of Independence Day in our Mexican-infused neighborhood.

My head is a truly happy place right now, where *what matters* matters less than *what doesn't matter*. In fact, I have no idea what matters at this point. But here's what doesn't matter: the *moral significance* of my mostly happy friendship with my neighbors.

Usually, I worry there's something shallow and sad and even wasteful about friendships built on principles no more rigorous than shared space. It's just not . . . strategic, somehow. Then again: *if you're not with the one you love, honey, love the one you're with.*

But once you truly do begin to love the one you're with, honey—then what?

Slowly, reluctantly, defensively, and still nervously, over the years I have come to (inconsistently) regard neighbors H., D., and E. as important people in my life. Newer neighbors M. and T., and erratic neighbor B. are also people whom I care about, whom I agonize about, whom I make sure I see not too little and not too much, whom I kick myself for getting too long-winded with, whom I plan adventures with, and whom I think about now as I'm thinking about myself and my life.

I'm terrified by neighbors, because I build boundaries so carefully and consciously. Neighbors make you do it on the fly.

Wanna come over for porch beers?

Wanna have a joint Super Bowl party?

Headed down to Costco in twenty minutes—wanna come along?

I prefer relationships with much more space and time to plan: *I think Thursday will work; let me check with my wife.*

I prefer relationships built on mutual interest or proven over decades: *We're writers. We're golfers. We're liberals. We're brother and sister.*

We're neighbors?

That's a little too explicit an assertion of the randomness of life for my taste. Except that . . .

Since we've been neighbors, we have developed some common interests—for example, most of us have motorcycles. And we've created a mostly makeshift institution whose rules none of us would violate—partly because we like each other, and partly because we wouldn't want to do anything to *fuck things up here.*

We've even given our little community a whimsically weighty name: Falconhead Manor.

The whole thing feels kind of gentle and noble to me.

It also feels like the kind of patriotism I can get behind: People suddenly stuck together by accident, careful not to tread on any toes. Conscious of the circumstantial nature of their association and governed in part by the very uncertainty of their bond. And usually enjoying, always tolerating, and occasionally really adoring one another.

Pride shouldn't come into it; we are just fellow travelers.

Arrogance shouldn't come into it; we are not "the best neighbors in the world."

Self-consciousness shouldn't come into it; in fact, this ought to be the last time I write about it.

Not usually one to make philosophical pronouncements, my neighbor H. stood beside the grill last night and said that when he was in the Air Force and moved every few months, he loved the changing vistas. Back then, he always imagined he'd live his whole life that way. But then he moved to Chicago, and he hasn't moved in more than ten years.

"I don't know," he said. "I'm just here. And I'm happy."
This seemed to come as a revelation to him, and he shrugged afterward as if to say: *What do you know about that?*

Not much, pal. Not much.

Except to say that it is a very happy July Fourth weekend.

Elder, Respect Thyself

Not only is it fashionable to reject the tried and true in favor of the untried and new—actually, that's what fashion is.

We live in a fashionable time. The problem is, the moment anyone over age thirty dares to share anything that sounds like advice, or wisdom accumulated from a life of trial and error (not to mention reading and thinking), it's *OK, Boomer*.

Actually, no. That's not the problem. It's not the response itself, but the *fear* of being accused of "mansplaining" that prevents older men *and* women from trying to teach younger people what we think we know. I don't mean what we know culturally; we middle-agers run corporations and the movies and the media, and we get our voices heard publicly and constantly. I mean in personal situations, family situations—in potential teaching situations that turn into a bitten tongue concealed by a kindly smile.

What's got me lamenting this is the best little essay I've read in a while, by the writer Rebecca McCarthy, about Norman Maclean, the late writer and University of Chicago professor who wrote the novella *A River Runs Through It*. The essay recalls McCarthy's teenage acquaintance with Maclean fifty years ago when the old professor was summering in Montana, where McCarthy lived. They met through a coincidental family connection.

Handed McCarthy's adolescent poems by a family member, the old man read them and told her what was good about them, "telling me things I had never noticed about their rhythm and language."

Seeing her order a Tom Collins before dinner—odd, I know, but so was Montana back then—Maclean later told her that's not how it's done.

> Before dinner, you can drink Scotch or bourbon, with ice or water or club soda. With a twist of lemon in the Scotch if you like. Or you can have a glass of sherry.
>
> A Tom Collins, a gin and tonic, those are drinks for you and your boyfriend after a game of tennis. Not before a meal. With food, you can have wine. And after a meal, you can have another glass of Scotch or bourbon. Or a sherry. Or a cordial, maybe brandy. That's it, darling, those are your choices.

And he told her that she was *not* to attend college in Montana, but rather the University of Chicago.

> "Fuck it, Rebecca," he said: "Chicago's the big leagues, darling, but I think you could handle it. You're a strong, powerful woman."
>
> Until then, no one had ever referred to me as a woman, much less a strong, powerful one. I felt older just hearing it and decided I would think of myself as a strong, powerful woman from then on.

Maclean himself had attended Dartmouth:

> "But the East isn't the place for you, Rebecca. The Ivy League is filled with rich men's sons and daughters. Old money. Secret societies. Joe College. Bastards."
>
> He shook his head and hissed, "Ssssttt." The sound was a cross between a punctured tire and an angry rattlesnake. "No, Chicago's the place for you, darling. A strong, powerful woman like yourself, a poet, they would love you."

The part about the school blew right over me. What I heard was that Norman considered me a poet. When an adult names you, before the wax is completely dry, the name becomes part of who you are.

Of course that's exactly what younger people and sensitive older people both fear—that influential adults *can* name you before the wax is dry, and what if they name you wrong?

But what if the elders in a society—those in our own family, our parents' friends, the old lady at the end of the bar who can see you're holding the pool stick wrong—don't dare to share their experience at all? We'll have to get all our wisdom from the internet, I guess.

But YouTube videos do not strong, powerful women make.

Healed for Life

I've got a question.

I ask it because I recently remembered in great detail an afternoon at our lake house, when I was about ten. It probably took place in the usual tense atmosphere—Mom (quietly) pissed that she had to pack the car and get a whole new array of groceries, Dad (quietly) pissed that Mom's such a damn baby, my little sister and I pretending not to know everything and feel everything.

But then our springer spaniel, Winner, took off after a squirrel. He was at a dead run when the chain ran out, and instead of flying up in the air, for some reason his head went down.

"It was like he went down in a hole!" my dad shouted, gasping. Dad could not get hold of himself after seeing Winner go down like that. Could not stop laughing. We were alarmed, until we started laughing too. And then we couldn't stop laughing either.

So we all sat down at the dining room table and laughed and laughed. When we started to stop laughing, we asked Dad when was the last time he'd laughed like that. He said there was a time—and he started laughing again just thinking of it—in maybe 1930, when his mother stopped the car on a country road to ask directions.

"Do you know how to get to Middletown?" she asked a farmer.

"No," the farmer replied. "How do ya?"

Dad said it was the funniest moment of his life. And he collapsed again, his whole body shaking, sounding like he was crying, and we all laughed like that, sitting at the dining room table, for maybe an hour.

The question is: We all know that some family incidents can scar us for life.

Is it also possible that other incidents can heal us for life?

The Painful Intimacy
of Saying *You're Welcome*

A friend of mine expressed her consternation at the reluctance of the "under-forty crowd" to say *You're welcome*.

Instead, it's *No problem*.

I have feelings about this, but they're not as much annoyance as sadness.

I think this discomfort with the traditional *Thank you/You're welcome* transaction betrays confusion about who we are, what we deserve to get from one another, and what we are responsible to give.

In the dark about all that, and thus afraid to owe or to be owed, we try to turn every interaction into a neutral trade. Every transaction is a "win-win." Every teacher learns just as much from the students. And every kindness wasn't a kindness at all. It was, instead, "no problem." Or, as a sweet-voiced Australian hotel clerk once said in words poetic to these ears of mine, "Not a worry, Meestah Murray."

I'd like to declare myself above this syndrome, but I fall prey to it too. For instance, I deliver a piece of equipment to a guy across town. When he thanks me, I say, "Oh, no worries. It was actually a nice motorcycle ride over here."

That is true.

But it is also true that he had apologetically asked a favor and had thanked me for doing it, and so it was my social duty to say, before *no worries* and the gracious motorcycle anecdote, *You're welcome*.

Most of us are better at giving generously than receiving graciously. But each of these acts, in healthy relationships and a healthy society, is as important as the other.

There Must Be
a Better Word Than *Grief*

Eulogies bother some people, who see them as the expression of empty niceties about imperfect people. To these people, eulogies seem like a kind of lie.

I think eulogies—especially good ones, which say things that are specific and true about what the person added to our lives—aren't a lie, but rather the truth by which we should always strive to live.

Far from being a sunny description of a malevolent person, most eulogies are usually pretty accurate accounts of the contributions, physical or spiritual, that a now demonstrably mortal person has made. After a lifetime of finding the person wanting—not bold enough, not hardworking enough, not sophisticated enough—now we see that the person is dead. And suddenly it seems that it would be not only impolite but *strange* to get everyone together and complain, in any but the most loving way, that Aunt Freda was a terrible cook, or that Dad couldn't change a tire if you gave him a three-lug-nut head start.

Now that someone is dead, it's an incontrovertible logical fact that the person did the very best he or she could. If the person had any redeeming qualities that we as individuals and as a community want to carry forth with us, it is those that we should spend a few minutes listing. And in the process, we find that most people, when they are dead, turn out to have had a longer list of admirable qualities than most of us made time to

consider while they were alive, when we were busy keeping an alphabet-
ized inventory of their shortcomings.

Perhaps we should strive to remember that shortcomings are nothing
more than the ways in which other people fall short of the ideal version of
them that our own powerful imagination has secretly and unfairly created
out of whole cloth.

Our more generous assessment of people in death should inform our
treatment of people in life. A few years ago, the sudden death of a vivid
and bright and difficult and troubled family friend took me back to the
death of my own mother, and I wrote this little thing:

> What do I know about grief? I know what everyone knows
> about it. And I've had a chance to see it lately, at close range
> and with sufficient remove.
>
> Grief should be called sadness-induced insanity.
>
> When you're grieving, every decision you make, you'll
> second-guess later, muttering, "What in the world was I
> thinking?"
>
> You will walk into a convenience store with a porcelain
> coffee cup in your hand.
>
> You will nearly get hit by cars, because your world has
> been so spectacularly destroyed that you can't believe every-
> one in Chicago doesn't know to stay out of your way. *They
> didn't know the Hindenburg exploded? Have they been living
> under a rock?*
>
> Grief might also be called "wisdom."
>
> It's in grief that some acquaintances become your friends,
> and some friends become your family, because you have been
> too distracted to sort those things out as you went along.
>
> My college roommate became my best friend one after-
> noon in the basement of our house shortly after my mother
> died, by shooting fifty games of pool with me and asking me

one hundred questions about what it feels like to have your mother die.

That very same week, it must have been, my girlfriend's mother became a mother of mine (and my mother-in-law eventually) by filling her wine glass all the way up, leaning back, and asking me, "So, tell me about your mother."

(That was a good week!)

Grief might best be called "God."

Grief demands truth from those suffering through it and from those hoping to help. It exposes their egos and their lies, white and otherwise.

Grief reveals everyone's limits—including those of the dead—and in doing so gives everyone one perfect, shining chance to forgive everyone for everything. (Everyone should take it.)

Grief reduces politicians and other celebrities to their properly plain status as Someone We Don't Love, and grief exalts Everyone We Do Love, dead and living, to where they belong—*up in the sky!*—for however long we remember to hold them there, together, despite their madness and limitations and clumsiness and bad timing and vulnerable points of integrity and unfair judgment that finds us wanting, too.

Wanting, and beloved.

Communicating with Yourself

Most of the talking we do, we do with ourselves.

The oral historian Studs Terkel wrote an autobiography called *Talking to Myself.*

Golfers, among other people, are always yelling at themselves by name. "Jennifer Davis!" my sister-in-law Jeni will yell as her ball rolls past the hole. Or "Jennifer *Jean* Davis!" if it rolls into the pond.

I once spilled my beer and called myself an idiot. My sister, a psychologist, excoriated me: "Don't say that! What if your inner child hears?"

Maybe the first time I really considered the idea of communicating with myself was when I read Henry David Thoreau, who said that the man who goes "constantly and desperately to the post-office . . . has not heard from himself this long while."

As if we are one thing, and our self is another. As if we can choose to listen to our self, or not.

This separate self is a familiar idea to a writer. "I don't know what I think," wrote Flannery O'Connor, "until I read what I say."

In fact, it's a familiar idea to all of us. Terkel loved to tell the story of a woman he interviewed with his tape recorder at a Chicago housing project: "Skinny, pretty, bad teeth—meaning no dental care—and the kids are jumping around, 'cause they want to hear their mamma's voice played back . . . and so I play it back, and she listens to what she said on the tape and she says, 'Oh my God,' she says. 'I never knew I felt that way before.'"

And it's more complicated than that. We are advised to *speak from the heart* . . . to *say what's on your mind* . . . to *be yourself.* Yet pretty early in childhood, we realize that our selves vary with the company we keep, and we're often of at least two minds. As my dad used to put it, "The heart has reasons that reason doesn't understand."

We each contain multitudes, and communicating with other multitude-containers is an undertaking more like magic than mathematics. Yet even professional communicators are likely to label a piece of communication either candor or spin, effective or useless, spot on or fake.

But that's not how communication works. At all.

Between the very occasional bald-faced lies and gleaming truths we tell are infinite varieties of sincerity.

If I say *I love you* to my daughter, it's more sincere than when I speak the very same words to my wife's uncle Johnny, isn't it? (Even though I *do* love the guy!)

If I say you wrote a "great" article, do I mean that in the same sense as *The Great Gatsby* is a "great" book?

Or what about *I am glad to be here.* While not entirely untrue, whether I'm standing before a big audience sweating my palms off or standing on the first tee of a golf course on the Fourth of July, the proportion and type of truth in those statements do vary. And yet you wouldn't have me stand up and tell the audience I'd rather be golfing.

Communication isn't a game of *she loves me, she loves me not.* At your very best, you're trying to be as honest as you can while still being as sensitive as you can and protecting your own interests and your loved ones' interests, too.

And you'll miss the mark almost every single time.

Forgive yourself, and do better next time.

Just like other people do.

Forgive them, and give them another chance, too.

Over and over again.

A half century ago, when Bobby Kennedy spoke about how we need to make an effort in this country, he was talking about making an effort to understand other people—the people we work for, the people who work for us, our political leaders, our colleagues, our family, our friends, and our fellow citizens of all kinds of backgrounds—at a moment of great national discord and disunity, mere hours after the death of Martin Luther King Jr.

Speaking publicly for the first time about his own brother's assassination less than five years earlier, he addressed an audience that he acknowledged might be "tempted to be filled with hatred and distrust." And he said, "I can only say that I feel in my own heart the same kind of feeling. I had a member of my family killed . . . But we have to make an effort in the United States, we have to make an effort to understand, to go beyond these rather difficult times."

And in an all-Black, poor neighborhood in North Indianapolis, Kennedy didn't pander to his audience by reading them some Langston Hughes poem, or even by reciting a line from Martin Luther King Jr. Rather, he spoke of the inspiration he found reading Greek poetry in the dark years after his brother's death. He spoke from his own heart, and trusted it would reach the hearts of others

"My favorite poet was Aeschylus. And he once wrote"—and here, Kennedy pauses for five seconds, so long it begins to seem as if he has forgotten the words. But he has not—"'In our sleep, pain which cannot forget falls drop by drop upon the heart until, in our own despair, against our will, comes wisdom through the awful grace of God.'"

And in concluding, Kennedy borrowed once more from the ancients.

"Let us dedicate ourselves," he pleaded, "to what the Greeks wrote so many years ago: to tame the savageness of man and make gentle the life of this world."

Let us dedicate ourselves to that.

Acknowledgments

When I'm reading a good book, I often skip ahead to the acknowledgments section.

It seems like a chance to get to know the author a little more personally, through words written for colleagues, friends, and family.

And then it's disappointing, as the heretofore original author resorts to clichés, offering their "incalculable thanks" to librarians for their "tireless" help, agents and editors for their "devoted" efforts, and spouses, inevitably at the very end of the piece, for their "patience."

I'm going to try to do a little better than that.

And I'm going to *start*, rather than end, with my wife, Cristie Bosch. We are college sweethearts, which doesn't mean that we have lived a storybook marriage. It means that I do not have any idea what it would be like to be an adult without her by my side. (Lucky for me, she doesn't either.) Take each other for granted? Yes, we sure do—and love and truth and loyalty too. If you can assume those things your whole life, it makes a lot else possible—writing a book being only one. Thank you, Honey.

My daughter, Scout, has been the Brand-New Person who has put to the test all my ideas about communication—watching, as my own dad put it in his book on raising kids, to see "how consistently, how courageously I handle their consequences." Now seventeen at this writing, Scout watches me harder than ever, as my dad also put it, "to see if I seem as right about things as we look at each other eye to eye as I may have seemed from the seat of a tricycle." And even when she sometimes finds me wanting, I'm grateful she's still watching. Because I sure love watching her.

My younger sister Piper, who grew up with me in the House of Communication that I describe in this book—and also in the House of Heavy Silence, which I didn't describe in this book. Piper told me not long ago that she reads my blog Writing Boots every day at lunch. It occurred to me to tell her that if she were the only person who ever read it, I would write it just for her. There is no one on earth whom I admire more, and whose respect I so require.

Friends: in them I'm not just rich, I'm *nouveau riche*. My parents were very private people with just a handful of friends, and that's how I expected it to be for me too. No. My life is like the Gatsby mansion, but all the party guests are intimates and it's getting late and I'm forever charging around trying to hug everyone before they leave. It's not pretty, dear friends, as you know. But who are we trying to impress?

I will say something about one friend whom I've also never been an adult without: my Kent State college roommate Tom Gillespie, who insisted on editing this book. After reading and incorporating his edits into the manuscript, I told him in an email, "I was amazed at how many of these essays (like, almost all of them) were influenced by our conversations over 30 years, about all these subjects: communication, friends, family, politics, work. You and I live such different lives, and come at many things from such different points of view, that if there's a truth that holds in your life and my life both . . . then it's a truth we can both have some confidence in. I learned most of what I wrote in this book by myself—at home, at work, in Chicago. But I think our relationship—probably more than any of the many other friendships that have also enriched my life and improved my brain—has given me the confidence of the convictions I've come to."

Now, what kind of acknowledgments section migrates from personal to professional? Well, I never knew the difference between the two anyway.

There are the people technically responsible for this book: those who helped shape this book, and design, market, and distribute it. Obviously

Kris Pauls, and the warm, gentle, candid, creative, tasteful, happy crew at Disruption Books: Associate Publisher Alli Shapiro and designer Kimberly Lance. But not just technically—spiritually, too. You may or may not have noticed while reading, but this is a very weird book. Most publishers don't like to work with stuff that's not like other stuff they've successfully sold. When I was young, I had an editor reject something I wrote because, she said, "It's neither fish nor fowl." From the moment she laid eyes on the proposal for *An Effort to Understand*, Kris understood the book—and, increasingly, its author—in many cases better than I did. She spent most of her unbelievably thoughtful work convincing me *not* to pound this square peg into the round hole of the self-help genre, or to apologize for all the things this book is not. That's the beauty of this book, Kris seemed to say with every email, it's both fish and fowl! Kris, your contribution may have been professional, but the gratitude I feel is personal grade.

Jason Green, my dear friend and legal advisor. This is not just to thank him for his work on my contract for this book but also for his help on other projects, including his livelihood-saving help in a battle to acquire my publishing company several years ago. Jason has taught me what a whole career of writing did not: that arguments logically argued in words clearly written can actually hold water—can hold up against money and intimidation and expediency. To a fellow who has written several millions of words to utterly unknown effect, this is a profound and hopeful idea. And if your *pro bono* work for me will never quite be repaid, know that its value will never be underestimated.

Mike King and Benjamine Knight are actually in the book. With his patient business counsel, Mike singlehandedly converted me from a writer into a business owner when I formed Pro Rhetoric, LLC. His constant help and humor and companionship have been crucial comforts to both Benjamine and me throughout: we don't call him "Panda" for nothing. As for Benjamine, trying to describe our relationship overwhelms me, especially because she is easily embarrassed. She can only be described using the most old-fashioned words: decency, nobility, fidelity, and responsibility. BK, you're from another time and place, and I know every day how lucky I am to work with you in this one.

Finally, I have to thank the late Larry Ragan. My lucky writing apprenticeship came at his little publisher of trade newsletters for people in public relations. That may sound dreary. But the company was a menagerie of obscure but serious writers just like the founder who had collected them. These writers—and also many, many of their readers—wanted to do more than make a humble living hacking out readable words. They believed they could make a better society by exemplifying and promoting clear, candid, moral communication. They became my mentors, and then they became my friends. And their friends became my friends, eventually turning Chicago into a small town for me, where all the people were smart and funny and wise and real.

The world too.

Three decades later—as head of the Professional Speechwriters Association, publisher of *Vital Speeches of the Day* and ProRhetoric.com, and a daily blogger at Writing Boots—I am surrounded by such people, thousands of them. And they're all doing the best they can, despite sometimes crushing bureaucratic resistance, to use communication to humanize the places where they work and live, and brighten the relationships with the people they work and live with. These communicators believe in me, which they have proved to me by pre-purchasing many copies of this book in advance and promoting it as if it were their own.

It is.

References

Life, Communicated

Norlin, George, "Isocrates, Speeches (English)," Perseus under PhiloLogic by the ARTFL Project at the University of Chicago, 2018, http://perseus.uchicago.edu /perseus-cgi/citequery3.pl?dbname=GreekTexts.

If You Know How It's Going to Turn Out, It's Not Communication

Saunders, George, "George Saunders: What Writers Really Do When They Write," *The Guardian*, March 4, 2017, https://www.theguardian.com/books/2017 /mar/04/what-writers-really-do-when-they-write.

In Communication, the Style Is Part of the Substance

Ruddy, Christopher, "Don't Like Trump's Bluster? Sometimes It Works," *New York Times*, May 4, 2017, https://www.nytimes.com/2017/05/04/opinion/donald -trump-foreign-policy.html.

"Civility" Is Not Communication

Fox, Margalit, "Alfred C. Snider, Who Promoted Healthy Debate as Just That, Dies at 65," *New York Times*, December 17, 2015, https://www.nytimes.com /2015/12/17/education/alfred-c-snider-prominent-teacher-of-debating-is -dead-at-65.html.

Talking with the Poor, and Communicating with the Rich

House, Charles H., and Raymond L. Price, *The HP Phenomenon Innovation and Business Transformation* (Palo Alto, CA: Stanford University Press, 2009).

Authenticity as the New Eloquence

Kusnet, David, Ragan Communications' Speechwriters Conference, Spring 2006.

Communication Is Action!

Burnett, Sara, "Chicago Mayor Apologizes for Teen's Death, Vows Reforms,"
  The Boston Globe, December 9, 2015, https://www.bostonglobe.com/news
  /nation/2015/12/09/chicago-mayor-apologizes-for-teen-death-vows-reforms
  /73gtSr6kyZYxtNA4BjSXEN/story.html.

Obama, Barack, "Transcript: Barack Obama's Speech on Race," NPR, March 18, 2008,
  https://www.npr.org/templates/story/story.php?storyId=88478467.

Emanuel, Rahm, "Rahm Emanuel Chicago City Council Address Delivered
  9 December 2015, Chicago, Illinois," American Rhetoric Online Speech Bank,
  December 2015, https://www.americanrhetoric.com/speeches
  /rahmemanuelcitycouncil9december2015.htm.

The Unbearable Weight of Gravitas

Walker, Rob, "In the Internet Era, Does Anyone Still Have Gravitas?" Yahoo!
  Finance, March 19, 2014, https://finance.yahoo.com/news/in-the-internet
  -era-does-anyone-still-have-gravitas-79971442109.html.

Once Upon a Time . . . A Story about Rhetorical Pink Slime

Gottschall, Jonathan, "Theranos and the Dark Side of Storytelling," *Harvard
  Business Review*, October 18, 2016, https://hbr.org/2016/10/theranos-and
  -the-dark-side-of-storytelling.

Van Uhm, Peter, "Why I Chose a Gun," TED, 2012, https://www.youtube.com
  /watch?v=LjAsM1vAhW0.

Carpenter, Liz, "How to Write a Speech," *Texas Monthly*, July 2003,
  https://www.texasmonthly.com/politics/how-to-write-a-speech/.

Reffkin, Robert, "Compass' Mission," Compass Real Estate, 2017,
  https://www.youtube.com/watch?v=p4N0AIt3FFM&feature=emb_logo.

Real Leadership

"Business Roundtable Redefines the Purpose of a Corporation to Promote 'An
    Economy That Serves All Americans'" Business Roundtable, August 19, 2019,
    https://www.businessroundtable.org/business-roundtable-redefines-the
    -purpose-of-a-corporation-to-promote-an-economy-that-serves-all-americans.

Follow the Leader?

Murray, David, "How to Admire Leaders Without Thinking They're Infallible,"
    The Atlantic, November 21, 2012, https://www.theatlantic.com/national
    /archive/2012/11/how-to-admire-leaders-without-thinking-theyre-infallible
    /265540/.

An Open Letter to the "Man in the Arena"

Roosevelt, Theodore, "Theodore Roosevelt's Citizenship in a Republic:
    The Man in the Arena," LeadershipNow, https://www.leadershipnow.com
    /tr-citizenship.html.

Our Leaders Have Plenty to Be Vague About

Clement, M. W., "Railroad Regulation: The Public Is Interested in Fair Treatment,"
    Vital Speeches of the Day VII, No. 10, March 1, 1941.

Capper, Arthur, "Let Us Keep Out of Foreign Wars: Kill the Lease-Lend Bill,"
    Vital Speeches of the Day VII, No. 10, March 1, 1941.

Hutchins, Robert M., "The Path to War: We Are Drifting into Suicide," *Vital
    Speeches of the Day* VII, No. 10, March 1, 1941.

"Because They Know, They Understand"

Heron, Alexander R., *Sharing Information with Employees* (Stanford, CA:
    Stanford University Press, 1942).

Other Life, Not So Far Away

Wong, David, "How Half of America Lost Its F**king Mind," Cracked.com.,
    October 12, 2016, https://www.cracked.com/blog/6-reasons-trumps-rise-that
    -no-one-talks-about/.

Do *You* "Vote Your Interests"?

Smarsh, Sarah, *Heartland: A Memoir of Working Hard and Being Broke in the Richest
    Country on Earth* (New York, NY: Scribner, 2018).

What's Really "Deplorable"? Taking Communication Out of Context

Reilly, Katie, and Hillary Clinton, "Read Hillary Clinton's 'Basket of Deplorables'
    Remarks about Donald Trump Supporters," *Time*, September 10, 2016,
    https://time.com/4486502/hillary-clinton-basket-of-deplorables-transcript/.

Talking about Money Is Talking about Feelings

Davidson, Adam, "Debunking the Myth of the Job-Stealing Immigrant," *New York
    Times*, March 24, 2015, https://www.nytimes.com/2015/03/29/magazine
    /debunking-the-myth-of-the-job-stealing-immigrant.html.

Elder, Respect Thyself

McCarthy, Rebecca, "Norman Maclean and Me," *The American Scholar*,
    December 2, 2019, https://theamericanscholar.org/norman-maclean-and-me.

Conclusion: Communicating with Yourself

Thoreau, Henry David, "Life Without Principle," *The Atlantic*, October 1863.

Burkeman, Oliver, "Oliver Burkeman Talks to Studs Terkel," *The Guardian*,
    March 1, 2002, https://www.theguardian.com/books/2002/mar/01/studsterkel.

About the Author

David Murray heads the global Professional Speechwriters Association and comments daily about communication issues on his popular blog *Writing Boots*. He is an award-winning journalist and is editor and publisher of *Vital Speeches of the Day*, one of the world's longest continuously published magazines. He is the author of *Raised By Mad Men*, a memoir about his advertising parents, and co-author of the *New York Times* best seller *Tell My Sons: A Father's Last Letters*.

The son of two writers, Murray grew up in Hudson, Ohio, and studied English at Kent State University before moving to Chicago to make his own writing life. He lives in Chicago with his wife, Cristie Bosch, and daughter, Scout Murray.